Better Homes and Gardens®

Dieting for One

© Copyright 1984 by Meredith Corporation, Des Moines, Iowa.
All Rights Reserved. Printed in the United States of America.
First Edition. Second Printing, 1985.
Library of Congress Catalog Card Number: 83-63303
ISBN: 0-696-01412-2 (hard cover)
ISBN: 0-696-01410-6 (trade paperbackk)

BETTER HOMES AND GARDENS® BOOKS

Editor: Gerald M. Knox
Art Director: Ernest Shelton
Managing Editor: David A. Kirchner

Food and Nutrition Editor: Nancy Byal
Department Head—Cook Books: Sharyl Heiken
Associate Department Heads: Sandra Granseth,
    Rosemary C. Hutchinson, Elizabeth Woolever
Senior Food Editors: Julie Henderson, Julia Malloy,
    Marcia Stanley
Associate Food Editors: Jill Burmeister,
    Molly Culbertson, Linda Foley, Linda Henry,
    Lynn Hoppe, Mary Jo Plutt, Maureen Powers,
    Joyce Trollope
Recipe Development Editor: Marion Viall
Test Kitchen Director: Sharon Stilwell
Test Kitchen Home Economists: Jean Brekke,
    Kay Cargill, Marilyn Cornelius, Maryellyn Krantz,
    Lynelle Munn, Dianna Nolin, Marge Steenson,
    Cynthia Volcko

Associate Art Directors: Linda Ford Vermie,
    Neoma Alt West, Randall Yontz
Copy and Production Editors: Marsha Jahns,
    Mary Helen Schiltz, Carl Voss, David A. Walsh
Assistant Art Directors: Harijs Priekulis, Tom Wegner
Senior Graphic Designers: Alisann Dixon,
    Lynda Haupert, Lyne Neymeyer
Graphic Designers: Mike Burns, Mike Eagleton,
    Deb Miner, Stan Sams, D. Greg Thompson,
    Darla Whipple, Paul Zimmerman

Vice President, Editorial Director: Doris Eby
Executive Director, Editorial Services: Duane L. Gregg

General Manager: Fred Stines
Director of Publishing: Robert B. Nelson
Vice President, Retail Marketing: Jamie Martin
Vice President, Direct Marketing: Arthur Heydendael

DIETING FOR ONE

Editor: Linda Foley
Copy and Production Editor: Mary Helen Schiltz
Graphic Designer: Darla Whipple
Contributing Photographers: Mike Jensen, Scott Little
Contributing Illustrator: Thomas Rosborough
Electronic Text Processor: Donna Russell

Our seal assures you that every
recipe in *Dieting for One* has been
tested in the Better Homes and
Gardens® Test Kitchen. This means
that each recipe is practical and
reliable, and meets our high standards
of taste appeal.

On the cover: *Stuffed Chicken Breasts*
(see recipe, page 27)

Contents

You're Number One

And don't forget it. Whether you're living alone and dieting or you're the only dieter in the family, you deserve the best. So here it is! Throughout this book you'll find a "de-light-ful" collection of single-serving, low-calorie recipes, developed and tested especially with you in mind. What's more, there are dozens of tips to help keep your diet on the right track.

To help you get the ball rolling, here's a sample of three main dishes for a full day of sensible eating. And there are lots more tantalizing, low-calorie recipes in the book to plan your daily menus. Before you know it, you'll be on your way to a healthier new you.

Granola-Berry Breakfast
(see recipe, page 73)

Burgundy Beef Soup
(see recipe, page 66)

Shrimp Creole
(see recipe, page 8)

Beef Chop Suey

281 Calories

¼	pound boneless beef top round steak, trimmed of fat	● Partially freeze beef; thinly slice across the grain into bite-size strips. Set aside.

3	tablespoons water	● Stir together the water and cornstarch. Stir in soy sauce, gingerroot, and beef bouillon granules; set aside.
¾	teaspoon cornstarch	
2	teaspoons soy sauce	
½	teaspoon grated gingerroot	
¼	teaspoon instant beef bouillon granules	

¼	cup fresh *or* canned bean sprouts	● If using canned bean sprouts, drain well. Spray a small skillet with nonstick vegetable spray coating. Add the onion and green pepper to the skillet. Cook and stir over medium-high heat for 1 minute. Add the bean sprouts and mushrooms to the skillet; cook and stir for 1 minute more. Remove all the vegetables from the skillet.
	Nonstick vegetable spray coating	
2	tablespoons chopped onion	
2	tablespoons chopped green pepper	
¼	cup sliced fresh mushrooms	

		● Add beef to skillet; cook and stir for 1½ to 2 minutes or till brown. Stir soy sauce mixture; add to skillet. Cook and stir till thickened and bubbly. Add vegetables. Cover and cook for 1 minute.

3	cherry tomatoes, halved	● Add tomato halves to the skillet. Cover and cook for 1 minute more or till heated through. Serve over shredded fresh zucchini. Makes 1 serving.
¾	cup shredded fresh zucchini	

Stir-frying is a good way to cook foods quickly. But watch out—the calories can climb if you use cooking oil (120 calories per tablespoon). Substitute nonstick vegetable spray coating and spare yourself the oily calories. Just remember to keep the heat at about medium-high and stir the food constantly to prevent burning.

Buying and Storing Gingerroot

Grated fresh gingerroot brings a sparkle to the taste of many dishes. This knobby root has an aromatic flavor that's uniquely different from ground ginger. Look for a piece with light brown skin and firm, pungent flesh in the produce section of the supermarket.

A little gingerroot goes a long way, so be ready to store it for future use. To store, wrap the root in a paper towel and refrigerate. For long-term storage, immerse peeled slices of gingerroot in dry sherry and refrigerate in a covered container for up to three months. Or, freeze unpeeled gingerroot and cut off what you need while it's still frozen.

Shrimp Creole

330 Calories

Pictured on page 5.

1½ cups water
4 ounces fresh *or* frozen
   shelled shrimp

● In a medium saucepan bring the 1½ cups water to boiling; add the shrimp. Simmer for 1 to 3 minutes or till shrimp turn pink; drain. Set shrimp aside.

2 tablespoons chopped
   onion
2 tablespoons chopped
   green pepper
1 tablespoon water

● In a small skillet combine chopped onion, chopped green pepper, and 1 tablespoon water. Cover and simmer for 3 to 4 minutes or till the vegetables are crisp-tender. *Do not* drain.

1 8-ounce can tomatoes,
   cut up
½ teaspoon instant chicken
   bouillon granules
¼ teaspoon sugar
¼ teaspoon dried thyme,
   crushed
   Several dashes bottled hot
   pepper sauce

● Add tomatoes, chicken bouillon granules, sugar, thyme, and bottled hot pepper sauce to the vegetables in the skillet. Simmer, uncovered, for 5 minutes.

1 tablespoon water
2 teaspoons cornstarch

● Combine 1 tablespoon water and cornstarch; add to skillet. Cook and stir over medium heat till the mixture is thickened and bubbly. Add the shrimp. Cook and stir 2 minutes more.

½ cup hot cooked rice
1 tablespoon snipped
   parsley

● Combine hot cooked rice and parsley. Serve the shrimp mixture over rice and parsley. Makes 1 serving.

Creole cooking was developed by the descendants of French and Spanish settlers in Louisiana and the Gulf States. In this low-cal adaptation of a Creole classic, we've combined tender shrimp with a seasoned tomato mixture and spooned it over a bed of parsley rice.

Huevos Rancheros

276 Calories

1 6-inch tortilla	● Brush tortilla lightly with water to make it more pliable. Press tortilla into a small individual casserole. Bake in a 350° oven for 15 to 20 minutes or till the tortilla is crisp.
½ of a 10-ounce can tomatoes and green chili peppers 2 eggs	● Meanwhile, in a small skillet bring tomatoes and green chili peppers to boiling; reduce heat. Carefully break the eggs into the skillet. Cover and cook the eggs over low heat about 5 minutes or to desired doneness.
2 tablespoons shredded Monterey Jack cheese (½ ounce)	● Carefully slide the egg and tomato mixture into the warm tortilla, as shown. Sprinkle with shredded cheese. Return to oven about 1 minute more or till cheese melts. Makes 1 serving.

We crisped the tortilla for this Mexican dish in the oven, rather than frying it in oil, to save you at least 200 calories.

Leftover tortillas? No problem, amigo! Just wrap them securely in a freezer bag and store in the freezer for another use.

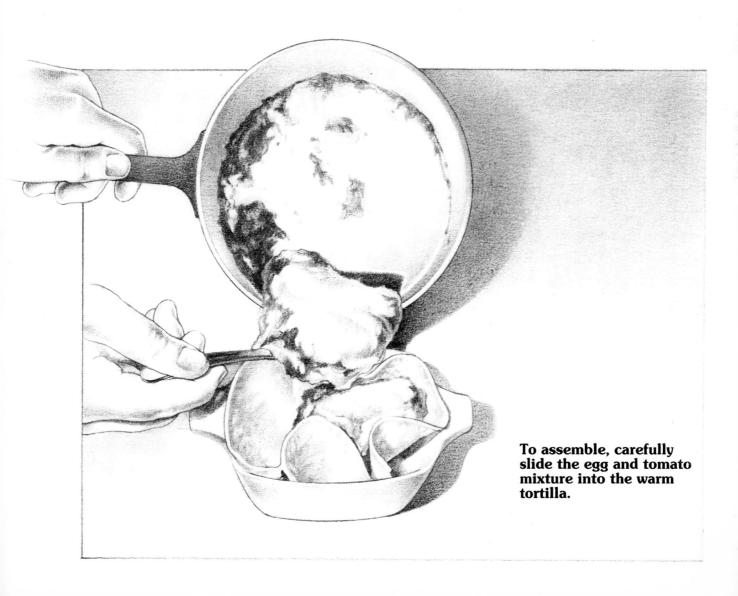

To assemble, carefully slide the egg and tomato mixture into the warm tortilla.

Open-Faced Beef Barbecue Sandwich

252 Calories

3 ounces lean ground beef 2 tablespoons chopped onion	● In a small skillet cook the lean ground beef and chopped onion over medium heat till the meat is brown and onion is tender; drain off fat.
¼ cup hot-style tomato juice ¼ teaspoon cornstarch ½ teaspoon prepared mustard Dash salt Dash pepper	● Stir together tomato juice and cornstarch; stir into the meat mixture in the skillet. Add the prepared mustard, salt, and pepper. Cook and stir till the mixture is thickened and bubbly.
½ hard roll, split and toasted ¼ cup shredded lettuce	● Place toasted roll slices, cut side up, on a small serving plate. Spoon the meat mixture over the roll slices; top with shredded lettuce. Makes 1 serving.

"It's so full! Why not serve it open-faced?" suggested a Taste Panel member. So here it is, as full and flavorful as ever. For about the same number of calories, you can substitute two ½-inch-thick slices of French bread for the hard roll half.

Factoring In Fiber

Fiber, sometimes called roughage or bulk, should play an important part in healthy, well-balanced meals. Here are a few practical tips to help you boost your daily fiber intake:

● Substitute a bowl of hot cooked oatmeal for your morning bacon and eggs.

● Whole grain breads should be your first choice for toast, sandwiches, croutons, and bread crumbs.

● Eat chili and soups with plenty of beans and vegetables.

● Whenever possible, leave the peel on fruits and vegetables such as apples, peaches, plums, carrots, tomatoes, and potatoes.

● Substitute garbanzo beans for part of the meat and cheese in a chef's salad, along with a light sprinkling of nuts.

● Sneak in a few nuts, dried fruits, and/or seeds to baked goods, meats, vegetables, and desserts.

● Grab a piece of fresh fruit for dessert instead of reaching for sweet treats.

● Spread a little fruit jam on your whole grain muffin instead of butter or margarine.

Potato Salad Vinaigrette

70 Calories

½ cup cubed tiny new potatoes (2 potatoes)	● In a small saucepan cook potatoes in a small amount of boiling water about 10 minutes or till tender; drain.
1 tablespoon low-calorie Italian salad dressing	● In a small mixing bowl combine salad dressing and drained cooked potatoes; toss gently to coat. Cover and chill mixture for at least 1 hour.
¼ cup chopped cucumber 2 radishes, sliced 2 tablespoons chopped green *or* sweet red pepper ⅛ teaspoon dried dillweed Lettuce leaf	● Before serving, toss the potatoes and Italian salad dressing with chopped cucumber, sliced radishes, chopped green or sweet red pepper, and dillweed. On a small plate spoon the potato-vegetable mixture onto a lettuce leaf. Makes 1 serving.

This crunchy, marinated potato salad tastes as good as it looks. Leave the skins on the new potatoes to retain the vitamins and add appeal.

New England Clam Chowder

224 Calories

1 6½-ounce can minced clams

● Drain clams and reserve liquid. Divide clams and the liquid in half. Place *half* of the clams and *half* of the liquid in a moisture-vaporproof container; freeze for another use. To the remaining clam liquid add enough water to measure ⅓ cup. Set aside remaining clams.

½ cup diced potatoes
1 tablespoon chopped onion

● In a small saucepan combine diced potatoes, chopped onion, and the clam liquid-water mixture. Bring to boiling; reduce heat. Cover and cook about 10 minutes or till the potatoes are tender.

⅔ cup skim milk
1 tablespoon skim milk
½ teaspoon cornstarch

● Add the ⅔ cup skim milk and reserved clams to the potato mixture in the saucepan. Combine the 1 tablespoon skim milk and cornstarch; stir into the mixture in saucepan. Cook and stir till the mixture is thickened and bubbly. Cook and stir 2 minutes more.

Few dashes Worcestershire sauce
⅛ teaspoon pepper
Dash salt

● Stir the Worcestershire sauce, pepper, and salt into the clam mixture in the saucepan. Transfer to a soup bowl. Makes 1 serving.

Instead of letting leftover clams go to waste, pack them along with the clam liquid in a small moisture-vaporproof container. Seal, label, and freeze till you're ready to make this hearty classic again.

Ratatouille-Style Vegetables

67 Calories

½ of an 8-ounce can
    tomatoes, cut up
1 small onion, sliced
½ cup sliced zucchini
¼ cup chopped green pepper

● In a small saucepan combine tomatoes, sliced onion, sliced zucchini, and chopped green pepper.

¼ teaspoon dried basil,
    crushed
⅛ teaspoon dried thyme,
    crushed
    Dash garlic powder
    Dash pepper

● Stir the basil, thyme, garlic powder, and pepper into the vegetables in the saucepan. Bring to boiling; reduce heat. Cover and simmer gently for 10 minutes. Uncover and cook about 10 minutes more or till the liquid in the saucepan is nearly evaporated.

● Serve hot as a vegetable side dish or chill and serve cold as a side-dish salad. Makes 1 serving.

Ratatouille (ra-ta-TOOEY) is a well-seasoned vegetable stew or casserole that originated in Provence, France. Our version takes the single dieter's needs into account—there is no high-calorie olive oil or hard-to-use-up eggplant.

Cut the Calories Yourself

You needn't deprive yourself of the pleasure of eating a favorite food just because you're dieting. Throughout this book are some delicious choices. To go a step further, reduce the calories in some of your own favorite recipes by following these cooking tips:

● Use lean cuts of meat trimmed of fat.
● Cook foods in a minimum amount of oil or use nonstick vegetable spray coating.
● Substitute plain low-fat yogurt for sour cream and substitute skim milk for whole milk.
● Thicken sauces with cornstarch instead of flour (1 teaspoon of cornstarch has the same thickening power as 2 teaspoons flour).
● Use water-pack and juice-pack canned foods instead of those packed in oil or heavy syrup.
● Substitute Neufchâtel cheese for cream cheese.
● Use herbs and spices to provide flavor without furnishing calories.

Little Lemon Cheesecakes

156 Calories per serving

⅓ cup graham cracker
   crumbs
4 teaspoons butter *or*
   margarine, melted

● Combine graham cracker crumbs and butter. Press mixture firmly onto bottom and all the way up the sides of four fluted tart pans or about ¾ inch up the sides of four muffin cups; set aside.

2 eggs
½ cup low-fat cottage cheese
2 tablespoons sugar
2 teaspoons all-purpose
   flour
½ teaspoon finely shredded
   lemon peel
4 teaspoons lemon juice

● In a small mixer bowl or blender container combine the eggs, cottage cheese, sugar, flour, ½ teaspoon lemon peel, and lemon juice. Beat on medium speed of an electric mixer till well combined, or cover and blend till the mixture is smooth.

Lemon peel, cut into thin
   strips (optional)

● Divide cheese mixture evenly among crusts. Bake in a 350° oven for 15 to 18 minutes or till center appears set. Cool slightly; cover with clear plastic wrap or waxed paper. Chill at least 2 hours. Garnish with lemon peel, if desired. Makes 4 (one-cheesecake) servings.

Did we goof? Nope! You *can* eat cheesecake on a diet, as long as it's our light and lemony version. With only 156 calories (compared to about 400 calories for conventional cheesecake), you'll have lots of rich taste but very few calories to look forward to at dessert time.

To store the cheesecakes longer, after chilling for 2 hours, place the cheesecakes, uncovered, in the freezer for 1 to 2 hours or till frozen. Remove from freezer. Place the frozen cheesecakes in a freezer bag and store in the freezer for up to 1 month.

168 Calories

Slim Eggnog

1 beaten egg yolk
¾ cup skim milk
2 teaspoons honey
¼ teaspoon vanilla

● In a small saucepan combine egg yolk, milk, and honey. Cook and stir over medium heat about 7 minutes or till mixture thickens slightly. Remove from heat; stir in vanilla.

Celebrate anytime with this rich-tasting creamy sipper. It saves you about half the calories of commercial eggnog.

Ground nutmeg

● Cover and chill. Before serving, sprinkle with nutmeg. Makes 1 serving.

Storing Cottage Cheese

Low-fat cottage cheese and dieting often go hand in hand. To enjoy cottage cheese at its peak, be sure to refrigerate it tightly covered. You'll have fresh-tasting cottage cheese for 7 to 10 days. Extend the freshness of the cottage cheese even more by turning the container upside down to help keep out air.

A word of warning—don't freeze cottage cheese. Freezing will change the texture of the cheese and cause it to separate.

To test fish for doneness, insert the tines of a fork into the fish; twist gently. The fish should easily break into flakes.

Fish and Vegetables à l'Orange

156 Calories

¼ teaspoon finely shredded orange peel
¼ cup orange juice
2 teaspoons soy sauce
¼ teaspoon grated gingerroot *or* ⅛ teaspoon ground ginger
1 medium carrot, cut into julienne strips

● In a small skillet combine the shredded orange peel, orange juice, soy sauce, and grated gingerroot or ground ginger. Add the carrot strips. Bring to boiling; reduce heat. Cover and simmer for 5 minutes. Push the carrot strips around the outer edge of the skillet.

Individual frozen fish portions are a real plus to the single dieter. Not only are they low in calories, but they make it easy to use just what you need without thawing the entire package of fish.

¼ of an 11½-ounce package (1 portion) frozen fish portions, thawed
¼ cup sliced zucchini

● Place fish in the center of the skillet. Arrange the sliced zucchini around the fish. Bring to boiling; reduce heat. Cover and simmer about 5 minutes or till the fish flakes easily when tested with a fork, as shown at far left. With a slotted spoon, remove the fish and vegetables from the skillet; set aside.

1 tablespoon water
½ teaspoon cornstarch

● Stir together the water and cornstarch; add to the orange juice mixture in the skillet. Cook and stir till thickened and bubbly; cook and stir 2 minutes more. Return fish and vegetables to skillet. Heat through, spooning glaze atop. Makes 1 serving.

Saucy Chicken and Cheese

190 Calories

½ of a 6-ounce jar artichoke hearts, drained

● Cut up any large artichoke hearts. Place the artichoke hearts in a small colander and rinse with *hot* water; drain well. Set aside.

1 teaspoon cornstarch
¼ teaspoon instant chicken bouillon granules
Dash salt
Dash pepper
¼ cup skim milk
½ cup cubed cooked chicken

● In a small saucepan combine the cornstarch, instant chicken bouillon granules, salt, and pepper. Stir in skim milk. Cook and stir over medium heat till the mixture is thickened and bubbly. Stir in the cubed chicken and artichoke hearts. Transfer the chicken mixture to a 10- or 12-ounce individual casserole.

1 tablespoon grated Parmesan cheese
⅛ teaspoon paprika
Snipped parsley

● Sprinkle the grated Parmesan cheese and paprika atop the casserole. Bake, uncovered, in a 350° oven about 10 minutes or till the chicken mixture is heated through. Sprinkle with snipped parsley. Makes 1 serving.

Why not save time as well as calories? Purchase frozen diced chicken meat and eliminate skinning, boning, cubing, and cooking your own chicken. Look for this convenient item in the freezer case at the grocery store and prepare according to package directions.

Polynesian Ham Patty

338 Calories

1 8-ounce can pineapple slices (juice pack)

½ of a 6¾-ounce can chunk-style ham, drained and flaked
1 egg yolk
1 tablespoon soft bread crumbs
1 tablespoon sliced green onion
1 tablespoon finely chopped green pepper
1 teaspoon Dijon-style mustard
  Nonstick vegetable spray coating

● Drain pineapple, reserving *1 tablespoon* juice. Cut *one* of the pineapple slices into eight wedges. Set aside. Store the remaining pineapple slices for another use.

● In a small mixing bowl combine the chunk-style ham, egg yolk, soft bread crumbs, chopped green onion, finely chopped green pepper, Dijon-style mustard, and the reserved pineapple juice; mix well. With your hands shape the meat mixture into 1 patty.

Spray a 7-inch pie plate with nonstick vegetable spray coating. Place the meat patty in prepared pie plate. Press the pineapple wedges into the ham patty to resemble spokes, as shown. Bake, uncovered, in a 350° oven for 20 to 25 minutes or till the ham patty is light brown. Makes 1 serving.

It's important for diet food to have eye appeal, and the fruit atop the ham patty is a simple, yet effective, way to do this. Firmly press the pineapple wedges into the ham patty to resemble spokes.

Hot 'n' Hearty Chili

327 Calories

4 ounces lean ground beef
2 tablespoons chopped
    onion

● In a small saucepan cook ground beef and chopped onion till meat is brown and onion is tender; drain off fat.

1 6-ounce can hot-style
    tomato juice
½ teaspoon chili powder
½ of an 8-ounce can whole
    kernel corn, drained
2 tablespoons bite-size
    shredded corn squares,
    coarsely crushed

● Add hot-style tomato juice and chili powder to the saucepan. Stir in the whole kernel corn. Bring to boiling; reduce heat. Simmer, uncovered, about 10 minutes or till heated through. Transfer to a soup bowl. Sprinkle with coarsely crushed cereal. Makes 1 serving.

On a blustery day, this robust dish will chase away the chill and any stubborn hunger pangs. Top it off with corn cereal for a crunchy contrast and a clever substitute for higher-calorie corn chips.

Choosing Ground Beef

All ground beef is not created equal. This is especially important to know when you're counting calories. For the fewest number of calories, look for *extra lean* ground beef, which contains approximately 15% fat (85% lean) and 214 calories for a 4-ounce serving. *Lean* ground beef contains approximately 25% fat (75% lean) and 261 calories for a 4-ounce serving. *Regular* ground beef chalks up approximately 30% fat (70% lean) and 284 calories for a 4-ounce serving. As a rule of thumb to remember when purchasing all red meats, the higher the fat content, the higher the calories, so choose the leanest meat available.

Puffed Brussels Sprouts Bake

251 Calories

1 cup fresh *or* frozen brussels sprouts *or* cauliflower flowerets ¼ cup water Dash salt	● In a small saucepan combine brussels sprouts or cauliflower, water, and salt. Bring to boiling; reduce heat. Cover and simmer for 10 to 15 minutes or till crisp-tender; drain. Halve sprouts or any large pieces of cauliflower. Transfer vegetables to a 14-ounce casserole.
1 egg yolk ¼ cup plain low-fat yogurt ¼ cup shredded Swiss cheese (1 ounce) ⅛ teaspoon ground nutmeg	● In a small mixer bowl beat egg yolk, yogurt, shredded cheese, and ground nutmeg on medium speed of a portable electric mixer till well combined. Transfer mixture to another bowl. Wash beaters and small mixer bowl thoroughly.
1 egg white	● In the small mixer bowl beat the egg white on medium speed of a portable electric mixer till stiff peaks form (tips stand straight). Fold the beaten egg white into the egg yolk mixture. Spoon the egg mixture atop the vegetables in the casserole. Bake, uncovered, in a 350° oven for 15 to 20 minutes or till puffy and light brown. Serve immediately. Makes 1 serving.

The crisp-cooked vegetables on the bottom of the dish are encased in a puffy cheese mixture that bakes to a golden brown.

When beating just one egg white for this recipe and other recipes throughout the book, we found it best to use either a portable electric mixer or a rotary beater, rather than a large electric mixer.

German-Style Skillet

376 Calories

4 ounces ground pork 2 tablespoons chopped onion	● In a small skillet cook the ground pork and chopped onion till pork is brown and onion is tender; drain off fat.
½ of an 8-ounce can sauerkraut, rinsed, drained, and snipped 2 tablespoons apple juice ¼ teaspoon caraway seed 1 small apple, cored and sliced	● Stir sauerkraut, apple juice, and caraway seed into the meat mixture. Arrange the apple slices atop the mixture. Cover and simmer about 5 minutes or till the apple slices are just tender. Makes 1 serving.

Apples, sauerkraut, and caraway team up with the pork to give this dish a distinctively delicious German flavor. Store the leftover sauerkraut in a covered container in the refrigerator for a slim and speedy salad or sandwich topper.

Barley and Cheese Soup

327 Calories

½ cup water
¼ cup bias-sliced carrots
2 tablespoons quick-
cooking barley
¼ teaspoon instant beef
bouillon granules
Dash pepper

¾ cup skim milk
2 teaspoons cornstarch
⅓ cup shredded American
cheese (1½ ounces)
2 teaspoons sliced green
onion

● In small saucepan combine water, carrots, barley, beef bouillon granules, and pepper. Bring to boiling; reduce heat. Cover and simmer for 12 to 15 minutes or till the barley is tender. Remove from heat.

● Stir together milk and cornstarch. Stir into barley mixture. Cook and stir over medium heat till the mixture is thickened and bubbly; cook and stir 2 minutes more. Add the shredded cheese. Cook and stir till the cheese melts. Transfer to a soup bowl. Before serving, sprinkle with sliced green onion. Makes 1 serving.

Don't be afraid to indulge in this rich and creamy meatless soup. One generous bowl gives you plenty of protein (thanks to the combination of dairy products and quick-cooking barley) without sabotaging your calorie allotment.

Cheddar and Rice Bake

327 Calories

1 beaten egg
½ cup cooked rice
3 tablespoons shredded cheddar cheese (¾ ounce)
2 tablespoons snipped parsley
2 tablespoons skim milk
Dash onion powder

● In a small mixing bowl combine beaten egg, cooked rice, shredded cheese, snipped parsley, skim milk, and onion powder; mix well.

Some foods, such as rice, are a bit tricky to scale down to one serving. We found that the most convenient way to get ½ cup of cooked rice is to use quick-cooking rice. Simply bring ¼ cup *water* to boiling in a small saucepan; stir in ¼ cup *quick-cooking rice.* Cover; remove from heat. Let stand 5 minutes. Drain, if necessary.

Nonstick vegetable spray coating
2 teaspoons sunflower nuts

● Spray an individual baking dish with nonstick vegetable spray coating. Spoon rice mixture into dish. Sprinkle with sunflower nuts. Bake in a 350° oven about 20 minutes or till a knife inserted near center comes out clean. Let stand 3 minutes. Makes 1 main-dish serving.

Pork Chops with Gingersnap Gravy

306 Calories per serving

4 pork rib chops, cut ½ inch thick 1 tablespoon cooking oil	● Trim excess fat from chops. In a skillet cook chops in hot oil on both sides till brown. Drain chops well on paper toweling. Place chops in four shallow individual baking dishes. Drain the excess fat from the skillet.
1¼ cups water 1 small onion, sliced and separated into rings	● Add water and onion to the skillet. Bring to boiling; reduce heat. Cover and simmer about 2 minutes or till the onion is tender.
¼ cup crushed gingersnaps (4 cookies) ¼ cup red wine vinegar 1 teaspoon instant beef bouillon granules ⅛ teaspoon ground ginger ⅛ teaspoon pepper Dash ground cloves	● Add gingersnaps, red wine vinegar, beef bouillon granules, ginger, pepper, and cloves. Cook and stir just till bubbly. Spoon the mixture over the pork chops. To serve immediately, cover and bake in a 350° oven about 35 minutes or till done. *Or,* place each baking dish in a freezer bag; seal, label, and freeze for up to 2 months. Makes 4 single-serving entrées.
	● **To cook 1 frozen single-serving entrée:** *Conventional Oven:* Remove baking dish from freezer bag; cover with foil. Bake in a 375° oven for 50 to 60 minutes or till heated through. *Microwave Oven:* Remove twist tie from freezer bag. Micro-cook in freezer bag on 70% power (MEDIUM-HIGH) about 5 minutes or till heated through, turning the dish once.

This is one way to eat cookies guilt-free while on a diet. Gingersnap cookies thicken the gravy that is draped over each succulent pork chop.

Ham and Mushroom Lasagna

305 Calories per serving

4 ounces lasagna noodles (4 noodles)	● Cook the lasagna noodles according to package directions; drain. Set aside.

1 cup ricotta cheese (part skim milk) 2 tablespoons skim milk ⅛ teaspoon pepper 2 cups sliced fresh mushrooms ¼ cup chopped onion 1 tablespoon butter *or* margarine	● In a small mixing bowl combine the ricotta cheese, skim milk, and pepper; set aside. In a medium saucepan cook the sliced mushrooms and chopped onion in butter or margarine for 4 to 5 minutes or till the vegetables are tender.

1 7½-ounce can tomatoes, cut up 3 ounces fully cooked ham, cut into thin strips 2 tablespoons snipped parsley ½ teaspoon dried basil, crushed	● Stir the *undrained* tomatoes, ham strips, parsley, and basil into the mushroom mixture in the saucepan. Bring to boiling; reduce heat. Boil gently, uncovered, for 15 to 18 minutes or till the liquid is nearly evaporated.

3 tablespoons grated Parmesan cheese	● Arrange ⅓ of the cooked noodles in the bottom of a 6½x6½x2-inch baking dish. Spread with ⅓ of the ricotta mixture and ⅓ of the mushroom mixture. Repeat layers of pasta, ricotta, and mushroom mixture two more times. Sprinkle with Parmesan cheese.

● Cover baking dish with foil. Place in the freezer for 30 to 60 minutes. Remove from freezer; uncover. Cut into quarters; transfer each piece to a greased individual casserole. To serve immediately, cover and bake in a 375° oven about 25 minutes or till done. *Or,* place each casserole in a freezer bag; seal, label, and freeze for up to 2 months. Makes 4 single-serving entrées.

● **To cook 1 frozen single-serving entrée:** *Conventional Oven:* Remove casserole from freezer bag; cover with foil. Bake in a 375° oven for 50 minutes. Uncover and bake about 10 minutes more or till heated through. *Microwave Oven:* Remove twist tie from freezer bag. Micro-cook in freezer bag on 70% power (MEDIUM-HIGH) for 8 to 9 minutes or till heated through, giving the dish a half-turn after 4 minutes.

Sounds too good to be low calorie, but it is! Triple-layered lasagna is oozing with tender strips of ham, sautéed mushrooms, creamy ricotta cheese, and much more. In addition, each serving is a whopping 295 calories less than traditional lasagna.

For the fewest calories, be sure to use ricotta cheese made from part skim milk (319 calories per cup) rather than ricotta cheese made from whole milk (401 calories per cup).

Stuffed Chicken Breasts

292 Calories per serving

Also pictured on the cover.

1 cup water ½ cup bulgur wheat ¼ cup chopped onion ¼ cup thinly sliced celery ¼ cup shredded carrot 1½ teaspoons instant chicken bouillon granules	● In a small saucepan combine the 1 cup water, bulgur, chopped onion, sliced celery, shredded carrot, and the 1½ teaspoons chicken bouillon granules. Bring to boiling; reduce heat. Cover and simmer about 15 minutes or till the bulgur is done. Remove from heat.
2 whole medium chicken breasts, skinned, boned, and halved lengthwise	● In the thickest part of each chicken breast half, cut a pocket about 3 inches long and 2 inches deep. Spoon some of the bulgur mixture into each pocket; reserve the remaining mixture. Secure the pockets with string or wooden picks.
2 tablespoons cooking oil	● In a large skillet cook chicken pieces in hot oil about 10 minutes or till brown, turning once. Remove string or wooden picks. Place each chicken piece in a shallow individual casserole. Divide the remaining bulgur mixture among the individual casseroles.
½ cup dry white wine ¼ cup water ½ teaspoon instant chicken bouillon granules	● Add white wine, the ¼ cup water, and the ½ teaspoon chicken bouillon granules to the skillet. Boil, uncovered, about 5 minutes or till the liquid is reduced to ½ cup. Spoon the liquid over chicken breasts. To serve immediately, cover and bake in a 375° oven for 5 to 10 minutes or till done. *Or,* place each casserole in a freezer bag; seal, label, and freeze for up to 2 months. Makes 4 single-serving entrées.
1 tablespoon snipped parsley	● **To cook 1 frozen single-serving entrée:** *Conventional Oven:* Remove baking dish from freezer bag; cover with foil. Bake in a 375° oven for 40 to 45 minutes or till done. Sprinkle with parsley before serving. *Microwave Oven:* Remove twist ties from the freezer bag. Micro-cook in the freezer bag on 70% power (MEDIUM-HIGH) about 7 minutes or till done, giving the dish a half-turn after 3½ minutes. Sprinkle with parsley before serving.

Don't cancel entertaining plans just because you're dieting. Invite a friend to enjoy one of these bulgur-brimming chicken breasts with you. And don't bother mentioning that it's low-calorie—no one will suspect it!

Use a teaspoon to carefully spoon about ½ cup of the meat mixture into each cooked manicotti.

Beef and Spinach Manicotti

273 Calories per serving

4	manicotti
1	16-ounce can tomatoes, cut up
¼	cup dry red wine
2	tablespoons tomato paste
½	teaspoon dried basil, crushed
¼	teaspoon dried oregano, crushed

● Cook manicotti according to package directions; drain. Rinse with cold water; drain manicotti again.

In a small saucepan combine the *undrained* tomatoes, dry red wine, tomato paste, basil, and oregano. Cook, uncovered, about 5 minutes or till the mixture is slightly thickened. Set aside.

Calorie counting doesn't mean dull eating by our standards. Liven up your meal with these tender pasta shells bursting with a savory meat filling. You can purchase large tube-shaped manicotti in almost any grocery store.

½	pound lean ground beef
¼	cup chopped onion
1	clove garlic, minced
½	of a 10-ounce package frozen chopped spinach, thawed and well drained
2	tablespoons grated Parmesan cheese
¼	teaspoon salt

● In a skillet cook the ground beef, chopped onion, and garlic over medium heat till the meat is brown and onion is tender; drain off fat. Stir in spinach, Parmesan cheese, salt, and ¼ *cup* of the tomato mixture.

● Spoon about ½ *cup* meat mixture into each manicotti. Place a stuffed manicotti in each of four shallow individual baking dishes. Spoon tomato mixture atop. To serve immediately, cover and bake in a 350° oven about 35 minutes or till done. *Or,* place each dish in a freezer bag. Seal, label, and freeze. Makes 4 single-serving entrées.

● **To cook 1 frozen single-serving entrée:** *Conventional Oven:* Remove baking dish from freezer bag; cover with foil. Bake in a 375° oven about 50 minutes or till heated through. *Microwave Oven:* Remove twist ties from freezer bag. Micro-cook on 70% power (MEDIUM-HIGH) for 7 to 8 minutes or till heated through, giving the dish a quarter-turn every 2 minutes.

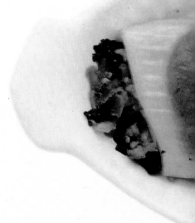

Place a stuffed manicotti in each of four shallow individual baking dishes.

Spoon the tomato mixture over the stuffed manicotti.

Place each baking dish in a freezer bag. Seal, label, and freeze.

Shrimp Mornay

331 Calories per serving

1 cup water
½ cup dry white wine
1 teaspoon instant chicken
    bouillon granules
¼ teaspoon dry mustard
    Dash pepper
	● In a saucepan combine water, dry white wine, instant chicken bouillon granules, dry mustard, and pepper; bring to boiling.

12 ounces fresh *or* frozen
    shelled shrimp
2 carrots, cut into
    julienne strips
4 green onions, cut into
    1-inch pieces
	● Add the shrimp, carrots, and green onion to the saucepan. Return to boiling; reduce heat. Cover and simmer for 1 minute. Remove shrimp and vegetables with a slotted spoon; set aside.

⅔ cup skim milk 2 tablespoons cornstarch 1 cup shredded process Swiss cheese (4 ounces)	● Boil the liquid in the saucepan, uncovered, for 5 to 10 minutes or till reduced to ¾ cup. Combine milk and cornstarch; stir into the liquid. Cook and stir till thickened and bubbly. Cook and stir 2 minutes more. Stir in cheese till melted. Remove from heat.
2 ounces linguine	● Cook linguine according to package directions; drain. Divide linguine among four shallow individual baking dishes.
1 cup frozen peas	● Combine peas, shrimp and vegetables, and cheese sauce. Spoon shrimp mixture over linguine. To serve immediately, cover and bake in a 350° oven for 25 to 30 minutes or till done. *Or,* place each baking dish in a freezer bag; seal, label, and freeze for up to 2 months. Makes 4 single-serving entrées.
	● **To cook 1 frozen single-serving entrée:** *Conventional Oven:* Remove baking dish from freezer bag; cover with foil. Bake in a 375° oven about 45 minutes or till heated through. *Microwave Oven:* Remove twist tie from freezer bag. Micro-cook in freezer bag on 70% power (MEDIUM-HIGH) about 5 minutes or till heated through, stirring the mixture once.

Melt cheese in a white sauce and you have French Mornay sauce. Our version preserves the creamy richness of the classic sauce with a fraction of the calories.

Salmon Cabbage Rolls

274 Calories per serving

1 beaten egg
¼ cup finely chopped onion
1 teaspoon Worcestershire sauce
    Dash pepper
1 15½-ounce can salmon, drained, flaked, and skin and bones removed
¾ cup cooked rice

● In a mixing bowl combine the beaten egg, chopped onion, Worcestershire sauce, and dash pepper. Add flaked salmon and cooked rice; mix well.

To remove the larger center vein from the cabbage leaves, use a sharp paring knife to cut along both sides of the vein, keeping the leaf in one piece.

8 large cabbage leaves
    Boiling water

● Cut out the heavy center rib of each cabbage leaf, keeping each leaf in one piece, as shown. Immerse cabbage leaves in boiling water for 2 to 3 minutes or till limp; drain on paper toweling. Place about ⅓ cup of salmon mixture on *each* leaf; fold in sides and tuck ends under, as shown. Place two rolls, seam side down, in each of four shallow individual baking dishes. Set aside.

1 cup frozen peas, thawed
⅔ cup skim milk
1 teaspoon cornstarch
¼ teaspoon dried dillweed
¼ teaspoon salt
    Dash pepper

● In a blender container or food processor bowl combine peas, milk, cornstarch, dillweed, salt, and dash pepper. Cover and blend or process till smooth. Transfer mixture to a saucepan. Cook and stir till mixture is thickened and bubbly. Cook and stir 2 minutes more. Pour the mixture over the salmon rolls. To serve immediately, cover and bake in a 350° oven for 25 to 30 minutes or till done. *Or,* place each baking dish in a freezer bag; seal, label, and freeze for up to 2 months. Makes 4 single-serving entrées.

Place about ⅓ cup of salmon mixture on each cabbage leaf. Fold in the sides of the leaf and tuck the ends under.

● **To cook 1 frozen single-serving entrée:** *Conventional Oven:* Remove baking dish from freezer bag; cover with foil. Bake in a 375° oven for 50 to 60 minutes or till heated through. *Microwave Oven:* Remove twist tie from freezer bag. Micro-cook in freezer bag on 70% power (MEDIUM-HIGH) for 9 to 10 minutes or till heated through, giving the dish a half-turn every 2 minutes.

Petite Poultry Loaf

317 Calories

1 beaten egg yolk
3 tablespoons soft bread crumbs
1 tablespoon sliced green onion
1 tablespoon water
1 teaspoon snipped parsley
⅛ teaspoon salt
Dash ground sage

● In a small mixing bowl combine the beaten egg yolk, soft bread crumbs, sliced green onion, water, snipped parsley, salt, and ground sage.

¼ of a 1-pound package (4 ounces) frozen ground raw turkey, thawed

● Add the ground raw turkey to the egg yolk mixture; mix well. Shape the meat mixture into a 4½x2-inch loaf. Place the loaf in a small shallow baking dish. Bake, uncovered, in a 350° oven for 25 to 30 minutes or just till done.

1 tablespoon cranberry-orange relish

● Drain off fat, if necessary. Spoon the cranberry-orange relish atop the poultry loaf. Return the loaf to the oven for 2 to 3 minutes or till the relish is heated through. Makes 1 serving.

Have the butcher at your store cut the package of ground raw turkey into four equal parts while it's still frozen. At home wrap each portion in moisture-vaporproof wrap; seal, label, and freeze. Then just thaw one portion of the turkey at a time to use in the *Petite Poultry Loaf* or any of the other recipes on pages 34-36.

Capitalize on the Toaster Oven

A toaster oven is more than just a toaster. You'll find it comes in extremely handy when you're preparing single-serving recipes. You can bake or broil many of your favorite foods without heating up the whole kitchen. Because toaster ovens vary, be sure to follow the manufacturer's instructions. Take special note of the preheating directions and the recommended baking utensils.

Chinese Meatball Salad

346 Calories

1 beaten egg yolk
2 teaspoons fine dry
   bread crumbs
¼ teaspoon onion salt
⅛ teaspoon grated
   gingerroot
¼ of a 1-pound package
   (4 ounces) frozen
   ground raw turkey,
   thawed

● In a small mixing bowl combine the beaten egg yolk, fine dry bread crumbs, onion salt, and grated gingerroot. Add the ground turkey; mix well. Shape mixture into 8 to 10 meatballs.

Nonstick vegetable spray
   coating

● Spray a small skillet with nonstick vegetable spray coating. Add meatballs and cook over medium heat about 10 minutes or till done, turning frequently. Drain the meatballs on paper toweling.

½ of a 6-ounce package
   frozen pea pods, thawed
¼ cup thinly bias-sliced
   carrots
2 tablespoons Honey-Ginger
   Vinaigrette (see recipe,
   page 76)

● In a small mixing bowl combine pea pods, carrots, and the Honey-Ginger Vinaigrette. Add meatballs; toss gently to coat. Cover and chill.

Leaf lettuce

● To serve, transfer mixture with a slotted spoon to a lettuce-lined salad plate. Makes 1 serving.

When eating *Chinese Meatball Salad*, do so Chinese-style—use chopsticks. You'll eat more slowly, savoring each pea pod, carrot slice, and turkey meatball. Eating slowly gives your stomach a chance to feel full before you've eaten more than you had planned.

Turkey Pita Pizza

338 Calories

¼ of a 1-pound package (4 ounces) frozen ground raw turkey, thawed
2 tablespoons chopped green pepper

● In a small skillet cook the ground raw turkey and chopped green pepper over medium heat till the turkey is light brown and the green pepper is tender. Drain off fat, if necessary.

⅓ cup pizza sauce
⅛ teaspoon fennel seed, crushed
Pinch dried oregano, crushed

● Stir pizza sauce, fennel seed, and oregano into meat mixture. Cook and stir for 1 minute more or till the mixture is heated through.

1 6-inch pita bread round
1 tablespoon shredded mozzarella cheese

● Halve the pita bread round horizontally, as shown. Toast one of the pita halves under the broiler about 1 minute on each side or till crisp. (Store the remaining pita bread for another use.) Spread the meat sauce mixture over the toasted pita bread half. Sprinkle mozzarella cheese atop.

● Place the pita bread with meat topping under the broiler; broil 3 to 4 inches from heat about 2 minutes or till the cheese melts. Makes 1 serving.

With a right blend of spices, you can transform ground turkey into a sausagelike topping. The toasted round of pita bread provides a crispy low-calorie crust for the saucy meat mixture and gooey melted cheese.

To make the crust, cut the pita bread round horizontally forming two halves. Toast one of the pita halves; wrap and store the other for another use.

Turkey Stroganoff

391 Calories

Nonstick vegetable spray
   coating
¼ of a 1-pound package
   (4 ounces) frozen
   ground raw turkey,
   thawed
½ cup sliced fresh
   mushrooms
¼ cup shredded carrot

● Spray a small saucepan or skillet with nonstick vegetable spray coating. Crumble the ground turkey into pan; add mushrooms and shredded carrot. Cook and stir over medium heat till the turkey is light brown and vegetables are tender.

¼ cup skim milk
½ teaspoon instant chicken
   bouillon granules
⅛ teaspoon dried thyme,
   crushed

● Add skim milk, chicken bouillon granules, and dried thyme to the turkey mixture; bring to boiling.

¼ cup plain low-fat yogurt
1 teaspoon cornstarch
½ cup hot cooked spinach
   noodles *or* noodles
   Paprika
   Salt and pepper (optional)

● Combine the yogurt and cornstarch; stir into the mixture in the saucepan. Cook and stir till thickened and bubbly. Cook and stir 2 minutes more. Spoon the turkey mixture over noodles. Sprinkle with paprika. Season with salt and pepper, if desired. Makes 1 serving.

Traditionally, stroganoff is made with beef and laden with a scale-tipping sour cream sauce for as many as 700 calories per serving. Here, turkey and yogurt replace the beef and sour cream for a rich-tasting spin-off of this once-taboo main dish.

Chicken Croquettes

342 Calories

Nonstick vegetable spray coating ½ of a whole large chicken breast (8 ounces), skinned and boned	● Spray a small skillet with nonstick vegetable spray coating. Add chicken to the skillet and cook over medium heat for 4 to 5 minutes on each side or till tender. Remove the chicken from the skillet. Set aside to cool. Finely chop the chicken.
2 tablespoons chopped celery 1 tablespoon water ⅓ cup skim milk ½ teaspoon minced dried onion ½ teaspoon instant chicken bouillon granules ⅛ teaspoon dried sage, crushed Dash pepper	● Add the chopped celery and water to the small skillet. Cover and cook for 4 to 5 minutes or till the celery is tender; drain. In a small mixing bowl combine the celery, skim milk, minced dried onion, chicken bouillon granules, dried sage, and pepper.
¾ cup soft bread crumbs (1 slice bread) 2 teaspoons snipped parsley	● Stir ½ *cup* of the bread crumbs into the mixture in the mixing bowl, stirring till the bread crumbs are thoroughly moistened. Add the snipped parsley and the cooked chicken; mix well. Cover and chill thoroughly.
1 teaspoon butter *or* margarine, melted	● In a small mixing bowl stir together melted butter or margarine and the remaining bread crumbs. Divide chicken mixture in half. With wet hands, shape mixture into two ¾-inch-thick patties or two 3-inch logs, as shown. Roll patties or logs in crumb mixture. Place in a small shallow baking dish. Bake, uncovered, in a 350° oven about 20 minutes or till heated through. Makes 1 serving.

Croquettes are typically fried in hot oil, but we took the slim way out and baked these to a golden brown. Bread crumbs give the moist chicken mixture a crisp coating.

If you'd like, dab a little sour cream on each croquette, keeping in mind that 1 tablespoon of dairy sour cream contains about 25 calories.

To make the croquettes, shape the chicken mixture into two ¾-inch-thick patties or two 3-inch logs. Roll the patties or logs in the crumb mixture.

Special Dinner For One

For a sure bet on a slim and satisfying meal, try this 400-calorie menu. While you're preparing the Asparagus-Capped Chicken Breast (see recipe, opposite), poach three apple slices in a small amount of boiling water. Next, toss together a fresh green salad and add whole grain crackers. Now set the table with your best dishes and treat yourself to a well-deserved, first-rate dinner.

Asparagus-Capped Chicken Breast

274 Calories

½ **of a whole large chicken breast (8 ounces)**	● Skin and bone chicken breast half, as shown at right and center right. Place the chicken, boned side up, between two pieces of clear plastic wrap. Working from the center to the edges, pound the chicken with a meat mallet, forming a rectangle about a ¼ inch thick, as shown at bottom right. Remove clear plastic wrap.
4 **teaspoons water** 1 **tablespoon soy sauce** ¼ **teaspoon grated gingerroot *or* dash ground ginger**	● In a small shallow dish or a 9-inch pie plate combine the 4 teaspoons water, soy sauce, and gingerroot or ground ginger. Place chicken in dish; turn to coat. Cover and chill for 1 hour. Drain chicken, reserving soy sauce mixture.
	● Place the chicken on the unheated rack in a broiler pan. Broil the chicken 3 to 4 inches from heat for 2 to 3 minutes per side or till the chicken is tender, brushing occasionally with the reserved soy sauce mixture.
¼ **cup water** 3 **fresh *or* frozen asparagus spears**	● Meanwhile, in a small skillet bring the ¼ cup water to boiling; add asparagus. Reduce heat; cover and cook about 5 minutes or till crisp-tender. Drain.
2 **tablespoons shredded cheddar *or* Swiss cheese (½ ounce)**	● Arrange the asparagus spears atop the chicken on the broiler rack. Sprinkle with the shredded cheese. Broil about 1 minute more or till the cheese melts. Makes 1 serving.

To skin the half chicken breast, firmly grasp the skin with one hand and anchor the meat with the other. Pull the skin away and discard.

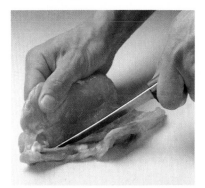

To bone the half chicken breast, place the breast bone side down. Using a sharp knife, cut the meat away from the bone, working from the breastbone side out.

Place the meat between two pieces of clear plastic wrap. Using the fine-toothed side of a meat mallet, pound lightly, forming a rectangle about ¼ inch thick.

Barbecued Liver

326 Calories

Nonstick vegetable spray coating
3 ounces beef liver

● Spray a small skillet with nonstick vegetable spray coating. Add liver to skillet and brown quickly on both sides; remove and cut into bite-size strips.

---

2 tablespoons tomato sauce
1 tablespoon water
1 tablespoon chopped onion
1½ teaspoons red wine vinegar
½ teaspoon brown sugar
½ teaspoon prepared mustard
½ teaspoon Worcestershire sauce
¼ teaspoon paprika
¼ teaspoon chili powder
½ cup hot cooked noodles

● In the same small skillet combine the tomato sauce, water, chopped onion, red wine vinegar, brown sugar, mustard, Worcestershire sauce, paprika, and chili powder. Return the liver to the skillet. Simmer, uncovered, about 8 minutes or till the liver is tender and still slightly pink. Spoon over hot cooked noodles. Makes 1 serving.

Although packages of beef liver come in many sizes, you'll most likely need to divide a package into one-serving portions. Opt for a 6-ounce package of liver so you can halve it to make _Barbecued Liver_ and _Sweet-and-Sour Liver,_ opposite.

Buying and Storing Liver

Liver is a smart food buy for the calorie-conscious cook. Besides being high in protein and relatively low in fat and calories (3 ounces of beef liver have only about 200 calories), liver also contributes iron, vitamin A, and B vitamins (riboflavin and niacin) to your diet.

When purchasing liver, choose meat that is fresh-looking and has a deep red color. Store liver in the refrigerator in its original wrapper and use it within two days. To store the meat longer, remove liver from its original package and rewrap securely in freezer wrap. Label and freeze the liver for 3 to 4 months.

Sweet-and-Sour Liver

396 Calories

½ of an 8-ounce can
(½ cup) pineapple
chunks (juice pack)
1 teaspoon cornstarch
2 teaspoons soy sauce
1½ teaspoons vinegar

● Drain the pineapple; reserve *2 tablespoons* of the juice. In a small mixing bowl combine the cornstarch and pineapple juice. Stir in soy sauce and vinegar; set aside.

Nonstick vegetable spray
coating
3 ounces beef liver, cut into
½-inch-thick strips

● Spray a small skillet with nonstick vegetable spray coating. Add liver; cook and stir over medium-high heat about 2 minutes or till the liver is tender and still slightly pink.

⅓ of a 6-ounce package
frozen pea pods, thawed
2 tablespoons chow mein
noodles

● Stir the soy sauce mixture; add to the liver in the skillet. Cook and stir over medium heat till thickened and bubbly.
  Stir in pea pods and pineapple chunks. Cover and cook about 2 minutes more or till pea pods are crisp-tender. Before serving, sprinkle with chow mein noodles. Makes 1 serving.

"What a pleasant surprise!" remarked one Taste Panel member who admitted to having a bias against liver. She sat down to this subtly sweet, mildly tangy stir-fry entrée and enjoyed an ample serving.
  To reduce the calories even further, you can omit the chow mein noodles and spoon the liver mixture over a bed of shredded fresh zucchini.

Fish and Spinach Salad Supreme

217 Calories

¾ cup water
3 tablespoons lemon juice
¼ of an 11½-ounce package
   (1 portion) frozen fish
   portions

● In a small skillet combine water and the 3 tablespoons lemon juice. Bring to boiling; reduce heat. Add frozen fish. Cover and simmer for 6 to 7 minutes or till the fish flakes easily when tested with a fork. Drain liquid. Carefully remove fish from skillet. When cool enough to handle, cut fish into bite-size pieces. Cover and chill.

Don't worry about what to do with the leftover frozen fish portions. You can use them in *Dilly-Lemon Fish Fillet*, opposite, or in *Fish and Vegetables à l'Orange* on page 17.

1 tablespoon lemon juice
2 teaspoons salad oil
⅛ teaspoon dried tarragon,
   crushed
— Dash pepper

● For the dressing, in a small bowl or custard cup combine the 1 tablespoon lemon juice, salad oil, dried tarragon, and pepper; set aside.

1 small clove garlic, halved
1 cup torn spinach
½ of a small onion, sliced
   and separated into rings
3 cherry tomatoes, halved

● Rub the inside of a small wooden salad bowl with cut garlic clove; discard garlic. Place spinach in bowl. Arrange the fish, onion, and tomatoes atop spinach. Stir dressing; pour over salad. Toss gently to coat. Makes 1 serving.

Dilly-Lemon Fish Fillet

139 Calories

¼ of an 11½-ounce package (1 portion) frozen fish portions, thawed
2 teaspoons lemon juice
Dash salt
Dash paprika
Dash pepper

● Place the fish portion in a small shallow baking dish. Brush the surface of the fish with the lemon juice; sprinkle with salt, paprika, and pepper. Bake in a 450° oven for 8 to 10 minutes or till the fish flakes easily when tested with a fork.

Cut the calories of the tangy dill topping even more by using reduced-calorie mayonnaise.

1½ teaspoons mayonnaise *or* salad dressing
1½ teaspoons plain low-fat yogurt
¼ teaspoon dried dillweed
1 cherry tomato, halved (optional)
Parsley (optional)

● Meanwhile, in a small mixing bowl or custard cup stir together mayonnaise or salad dressing, low-fat yogurt, and dried dillweed. Spoon over fish. Garnish with the cherry tomato halves and parsley, if desired. Makes 1 serving.

Cooking Fish

If you're in the market for an excellent quick-cooking, low-calorie main dish, then fish is it. Whether broiled, baked, steamed, or poached, fish come through on your diet with flying colors. To determine which cooking method to use, check the fat content of the fish. "Fat" fish, such as lake trout, whitefish, mackerel, salmon, and tuna, have oil throughout the flesh and are best broiled or baked because their fat helps prevent drying out during cooking. "Lean" fish, such as catfish, perch, cod, flounder, sole, and red snapper, have a drier flesh and generally are steamed or poached to keep the flesh moist.

Chicken and Brown Rice Pepper

318 Calories

1 medium green pepper	● Cut top from green pepper; discard seeds and membrane. Chop enough of the top to make 2 tablespoons; set aside. Cook the whole green pepper, uncovered, in boiling water for 5 minutes; invert on paper toweling to drain well.
Nonstick vegetable spray coating 2 tablespoons chopped onion	● Spray a small skillet with nonstick vegetable spray coating. Add the onion and reserved chopped green pepper to the skillet. Cook and stir over medium heat till the vegetables are tender.
1 small tomato, chopped ¼ cup water 2 tablespoons quick-cooking brown rice ¼ teaspoon instant chicken bouillon granules 1 small bay leaf Pinch dried thyme	● Add chopped tomato, the ¼ cup water, quick-cooking brown rice, instant chicken bouillon granules, bay leaf, and thyme to the skillet. Bring to boiling; reduce heat. Cover and cook for 15 to 18 minutes or till the rice is tender. Remove bay leaf.
⅓ cup cubed cooked chicken 3 tablespoons shredded cheddar cheese (¾ ounce)	● Stir the cooked chicken and shredded cheddar cheese into the rice mixture. Spoon the chicken-rice mixture into the green pepper.
	● Place the green pepper in a small shallow baking dish; cover with foil. Bake in a 350° oven for 30 to 35 minutes or till the green pepper is tender and the chicken-rice mixture is heated through. Makes 1 serving.

How can you tell when rice is really cooked? Squeeze a few grains between your thumb and forefinger. If there's no hard core, the rice is done.

Mediterranean Stuffed Meat Patty

345 Calories

2 cups fresh torn spinach
1 tablespoon water
1 tablespoon low-fat cottage
   cheese
1 tablespoon crumbled feta
   cheese
	● Place spinach and water in small saucepan. Cover and cook over low heat for 3 to 5 minutes or till tender. Drain spinach well. In a small mixing bowl combine cottage cheese, feta cheese, and spinach; mix well. Set aside.

4 ounces ground pork
1 small green onion, finely
   chopped
⅛ teaspoon garlic salt
   Dash pepper
	● In another small mixing bowl combine ground pork, green onion, garlic salt, and pepper; mix well. On waxed paper shape the meat mixture into two ¼-inch-thick patties. Spoon the spinach mixture atop one of the meat patties to within ½ inch of the edge. Top with the second meat patty, as shown, and press the edges together to seal.

	● Grill the stuffed meat patty over *medium* coals to desired doneness, turning once (allow 12 to 15 minutes total time for medium). *Or,* place patty on rack of unheated broiler pan. Broil 3 inches from heat to desired doneness, turning once (allow about 10 minutes total time for medium).
2 tablespoons tomato sauce 1 tablespoon dry red wine 2 teaspoons chopped green pepper	● Meanwhile, in a small saucepan combine tomato sauce, dry red wine, and green pepper. Bring to boiling; reduce heat. Simmer, uncovered, for 3 minutes. Spoon tomato mixture over meat patty. Makes 1 serving.

Using fresh spinach gives this burger a brilliant color and flavor. If fresh spinach isn't available, though, drain and chop half of a 7½-ounce can of spinach.

To stuff the burger, spoon the spinach mixture atop one of the patties to within ½ inch of the edge. Top with the second patty and press the edges together to seal.

Ham-and-Fruit-Salad Puff

Pictured on page 57.

265 Calories

½ of an 8-ounce can (½ cup) crushed pineapple (juice pack)
1 tablespoon plain low-fat yogurt
¼ teaspoon finely shredded orange peel

● Drain the crushed pineapple, reserving *1 teaspoon* juice. In a small mixing bowl stir together the plain low-fat yogurt, shredded orange peel, and the reserved pineapple juice.

An edible cream puff "bowl" makes this hearty ham, pineapple, and grape salad fun to eat.

⅓ cup diced fully cooked ham
¼ cup halved green grapes

● Combine ham, grapes, and pineapple. Fold in the yogurt mixture, tossing lightly to coat. Cover and chill.

1 Puff Shell (see recipe, page 56)

● Just before serving, spoon the ham and fruit mixture into the Puff Shell. Makes 1 serving.

Tuna-Tater Cheese Melt

276 Calories

1 medium baking potato

● Scrub potato thoroughly and prick with a fork. Bake in a 425° oven for 40 to 60 minutes or till tender.
  Cut a lengthwise slice from the top of the potato; discard skin from slice. Place potato portion from the slice in a small mixing bowl. Scoop out the inside of the potato, leaving a ¼-inch-thick shell; reserve shell. Add the insides of the potato to the mixing bowl containing the potato portion from the top slice; mash.

When you're in a hurry, micro-cook this main dish in next to no time. Prepare the recipe as directed, *except* place the raw potato in a shallow baking dish and micro-cook on 100% power (HIGH) for 3 to 5 minutes or till tender; let stand 5 minutes. Continue as directed at left. After piling the tuna filling into the potato shell, micro-cook on 100% power (HIGH) for 1 to 2½ minutes or till heated through. Sprinkle with cheese and paprika and micro-cook on 100% power (HIGH) for 30 seconds or till the cheese melts.

2 tablespoons skim milk
1 3¼- *or* 3½-ounce can tuna (water pack), drained and flaked
3 small ripe olives, chopped
1 tablespoon snipped chives

● Add skim milk to the mashed potato; stir till well combined. Fold in tuna, ripe olives, and chives. Pile the mashed potato mixture into the reserved potato shell. Place the potato in a shallow baking dish.

1 tablespoon shredded cheddar cheese
Dash paprika

● Bake the filled potato, uncovered, in a 425° oven about 25 minutes or till heated through. Sprinkle with shredded cheese and paprika. Bake for 2 to 3 minutes more or till the cheese melts. Makes 1 serving.

To make the tomato shell, core the tomato. With the base of the tomato up, cut the tomato into six wedges, cutting to, but not through, the stem end of the tomato.

After cutting the tomato into wedges, spread the wedges apart slightly.

To serve, place the tomato shell on a lettuce-lined salad plate. Spoon the egg-salad mixture into the tomato shell.

Tomato and Egg Salad Olé

264 Calories

2 hard-cooked eggs,
  chopped
⅓ cup low-fat cottage cheese
1 canned green chili pepper,
  rinsed, seeded, and
  chopped
1 tablespoon chopped
  pimiento
2 teaspoons sliced green
  onion
¼ teaspoon chili powder
  Few dashes bottled hot
  pepper sauce
  Dash garlic salt

● In a small mixing bowl combine the hard-cooked eggs, cottage cheese, green chili pepper, chopped pimiento, sliced green onion, chili powder, hot pepper sauce, and garlic salt; stir till well combined. Cover and chill.

Pile this chili-peppered egg salad high into a festive tomato shell for an easy entrée that packs a hot and spicy punch.
  Create a crunchy salad the next time around by spooning the filling into a crisp taco shell.

1 medium tomato

● For the tomato shell, core the tomato. With the base of the tomato up, cut the tomato into six wedges, cutting to, but not through, the stem end of the tomato. Spread the tomato wedges apart slightly.

Lettuce leaf
Coarsely ground pepper

● To serve, place the tomato shell on a lettuce-lined salad plate. Spoon the egg-salad mixture into the tomato shell. Sprinkle the filled tomato with coarsely ground pepper. Makes 1 serving.

Vegetable and Cheese Beef Cup

324 Calories

4 ounces lean ground beef 1 tablespoon snipped parsley ¼ teaspoon onion salt	● In a small mixing bowl combine the ground beef, snipped parsley, and onion salt; mix well. Press meat mixture onto the bottom and about 1½ inches up the sides of a 10-ounce custard cup, as shown at top right, making the beef cup about ¼ inch thick. Place the custard cup on a baking sheet. Bake in a 350° oven about 15 minutes or till done; drain off fat. Keep warm.
⅓ cup frozen mixed vegetables	● Meanwhile, cook the frozen mixed vegetables according to package directions; drain.
¼ cup skim milk ½ teaspoon cornstarch Dash pepper 2 tablespoons shredded American *or* process Swiss cheese (½ ounce)	● In a small saucepan stir together skim milk, cornstarch, and pepper. Cook and stir over medium heat till the mixture is thickened and bubbly. Stir in shredded cheese. Cook and stir till the cheese melts. Add cooked vegetables. Cook and stir for 1 minute more or till vegetables are heated through.
Paprika	● Remove the meat from the custard cup. Place the beef cup on a serving plate. Spoon the vegetable mixture into beef cup, as shown at bottom right. Sprinkle with paprika. Makes 1 serving.

To make the beef cup, press the meat mixture onto the bottom and about 1½ inches up the sides of a 10-ounce custard cup, making the beef cup ¼ inch thick.

To serve, carefully remove the cooked beef cup from the custard cup; place it on a serving plate. Spoon the vegetable mixture into the beef cup.

Apple and Cinnamon Squash

147 Calories

1 1-pound acorn squash	● With a sharp knife cut the acorn squash in half crosswise. Scoop out the seeds and strings; discard seeds and strings. Wrap one of the squash halves in clear plastic wrap; store in the refrigerator for another use. Place the remaining squash half, cut side down, in a small baking dish. Bake in a 350° oven for 35 to 45 minutes or till the squash is tender. Scoop out the pulp, leaving a ½-inch shell; reserve the squash shell.	**Make this side dish quick-as-a-wink in your microwave oven. Prepare the recipe as directed, *except* place the squash half, cut side down, in a small baking dish. Micro-cook on 100% power (HIGH) for 6 to 8 minutes or till the squash is tender, turning the dish once. Let stand 5 minutes. Continue as directed at left. After filling the squash shell with the apple-squash mixture, micro-cook on 100% power (HIGH) for 1½ to 2 minutes or till heated through.**

1   small apple, cored and
    finely chopped
⅛ teaspoon ground
    cinnamon
	● Place the squash pulp in a small mixing bowl; mash the pulp. Add the chopped apple and ground cinnamon to the mashed pulp; stir till well combined.	

	● Spoon squash mixture into reserved squash shell. Place the filled squash in the small baking dish. Bake, uncovered, in a 350° oven for 25 to 30 minutes or till heated through. Makes 1 serving.	

Stuffed Melon Salad

177 Calories

1   tablespoon plain low-fat
    yogurt
1   tablespoon frozen
    whipped dessert
    topping, thawed
	● In a small mixing bowl stir together the plain low-fat yogurt and whipped dessert topping.	**The rough netted skin on a cantaloupe makes it resemble a large nutmeg pod—hence, its nickname "nutmeg melon."**
		  Store the remaining cantaloupe half in the refrigerator. Be sure to cover the fruit tightly with clear plastic wrap to keep it from drying and to prevent other foods from absorbing its aroma.

¼ cup red grapes, halved
    and seeded
1   tablespoon chopped
    celery
1   tablespoon chopped
    walnuts
	● Add the red grapes, chopped celery, and chopped walnuts to the yogurt mixture in the bowl. Toss till the mixture is well coated.	

½ of a small cantaloupe Ground nutmeg	● Remove seeds from the cantaloupe. Spoon the fruit mixture into the center of the cantaloupe. Sprinkle with nutmeg. Makes 1 serving.	

Shrimp Salad Pocket

173 Calories

2 ounces frozen cooked shrimp (½ cup)
2 tablespoons frozen deluxe tiny peas
2 tablespoons chopped green *or* sweet red pepper
2 tablespoons low-calorie creamy cucumber salad dressing
½ teaspoon lemon juice
⅛ teaspoon dried thyme, crushed

● Thaw and coarsely chop the frozen cooked shrimp. Thaw the frozen peas. In a small mixing bowl combine the coarsely chopped shrimp, tiny peas, chopped green or sweet red pepper, low-calorie creamy cucumber salad dressing, lemon juice, and dried thyme. Stir till the mixture is well combined.

Pack a pita full of this shrimp salad and be the envy of the office at lunch time. Keep the filling separate from the bread and store it in a refrigerator at work till you're ready to eat. Or, place the filling in a vacuum bottle or insulated lunch box with a freezer pack before leaving home.

½ cup shredded lettuce

● Add shredded lettuce to the shrimp mixture in the mixing bowl; toss to mix.

1 6-inch pita bread round

● Cut the pita bread round in half, forming two pockets. Wrap one of the pockets in clear plastic wrap and store for another use. Spoon the shrimp mixture into the remaining pita pocket. Makes 1 serving.

Tuna-Tomato Salad on Lettuce

179 Calories

1 3¼- *or* 3½-ounce can tuna (water pack), drained and flaked ½ of a small tomato, chopped 2 tablespoons sliced green onion	● In a small mixing bowl combine the tuna, chopped tomato, and sliced green onion; mix well.
1 tablespoon reduced-calorie cucumber *or* buttermilk salad dressing ⅛ teaspoon dried tarragon, crushed	● Stir salad dressing and tarragon into the tuna mixture; mix well.
1 small head lettuce	● Slice off and discard the core end of the lettuce head. Cut another crosswise slice that is ½ inch thick. Cover and store the remaining lettuce in the refrigerator for another use. Place the lettuce on a salad plate. Spoon tuna mixture onto lettuce. Makes 1 serving.

Stack a crisp wedge of lettuce with fresh-tasting tuna, chopped tomato, sliced green onion, and a spoonful of tarragon-flavored dressing. Why choose ordinary tuna salads that border close to 300 calories per serving when you can get all this for less?

Reading the Labels

Differentiating between foods labeled *low-calorie, reduced-calorie,* and *diet* or *dietetic* isn't always easy. Here's a guide to ease the confusion when you shop.

A *low-calorie* food or beverage cannot contain more than 40 calories per serving and must bear complete nutrition labeling, according to regulations by the Food and Drug Administration (FDA).

Reduced-calorie foods must be at least one-third lower in calories and similar in taste, smell, and texture to the standard version of the same food. The FDA also requires them to include nutrition labeling.

Diet or *dietetic* can only appear on a label along with a low-calorie or reduced-calorie claim or when the food is useful for a specific dietery purpose, such as low-sodium diets.

Trim Turkey Bagelwich

208 Calories

½ of a split bagel
2 teaspoons reduced-calorie French-style, buttermilk, cucumber, *or* Italian salad dressing

1 spinach *or* lettuce leaf
2 1-ounce slices cooked turkey *or* chicken
4 thin slices of cucumber
2 thin slices of tomato

With a sharp knife, cut the split bagel half in half horizontally.

● With a sharp knife cut the split bagel half in half horizontally, as shown. Toast the bagel slices. Spread salad dressing over a cut side of each bagel slice.

● Top one of the bagel slices with the spinach or lettuce leaf, turkey or chicken slices, cucumber slices, and tomato slices. Top with the other toasted bagel slice. Makes 1 serving.

This calorie-saving trick is the greatest thing since sliced bread. Cut the bagel half in half again and use the slices in place of 2 regular slices of bread. You can use bagels in the same way with other sandwich fillings, or toast some bagel slices in the morning and spread with your favorite low-sugar jelly.

For the puff shells, drop the batter by small teaspoonfuls inside the prepared tart pans. Then spread the batter to cover the bottom and ¼ inch up the sides of each tart pan.

For the cream puffs, drop batter by tablespoonfuls 3 inches apart onto a prepared baking sheet.

Cream Puffs and Puff Shells

99 Calories per serving

2 tablespoons butter *or* margarine **½ cup water** **½ cup all-purpose flour**	● In a small saucepan melt butter or margarine. Add water; bring to boiling. Add flour all at once; stir vigorously. Cook and stir till the mixture forms a ball that does not separate. Remove from heat; cool slightly, about 5 minutes.
2 eggs	● Add eggs to saucepan one at a time, beating with a wooden spoon after each for 1 to 2 minutes or till smooth.
Nonstick vegetable spray coating	● *For the cream puffs,* spray a baking sheet with nonstick vegetable spray coating. Drop batter by tablespoonfuls 3 inches apart onto the baking sheet, making six mounds. Bake in a 400° oven about 30 minutes or till golden brown and puffy. Remove from oven; split the puffs, removing any soft dough inside. Cool on a wire rack.
	● *For puff shells,* spray six 5-inch tart pans with nonstick vegetable spray coating. Drop batter by small teaspoonfuls inside the tart pans. With a spoon evenly spread batter to cover the bottom and ¼ inch up the sides of each tart pan. Bake in a 400° oven about 20 minutes or till golden brown and puffy. Remove from oven; cool on a wire rack. Makes 6 cream puffs or puff shells.

Cream puffs make great edible containers for everything from salads to desserts. Try them in *Mini-Cal Mocha Puff, Garden Cheese Puff,* or *Ham-and-Fruit-Salad Puff.*

Whether you make six cream puffs, six puff shells, or a combination of each, store them in a freezer bag and freeze them till needed. Thaw puffs or puff shells, uncovered, at room temperature about 10 minutes.

Ham-and-Fruit-Salad Puff
(see recipe, page 47)

After baking, cool both the cream puffs and the puff shells. To keep the cream puffs crisp, split them while they're warn and remove any soft dough inside.

Mini-Cal Mocha Puff
(see recipe, page 88)

Garden Cheese Puff
(see recipe, page 58)

Garden Cheese Puff

213 Calories

Pictured on page 57.

½ cup low-fat cottage
   cheese, drained
¼ cup chopped tomato
2 tablespoons chopped
   dill pickle
½ teaspoon Dijon-style
   mustard
⅛ teaspoon celery seed

● In a small mixing bowl combine the low-fat cottage cheese, chopped tomato, chopped dill pickle, Dijon-style mustard, and celery seed; mix well.

Draining the cottage cheese helps prevent this open-facer from being a little on the soggy side.

1 Cream Puff (see recipe,
   page 56), split
   Lettuce leaf (optional)

● Spoon cheese mixture into the split cream puff halves. Serve the filled cream puff open-faced on a small lettuce-lined salad plate, if desired. Makes 1 serving.

How Small is Small?

When you're cooking for one, regular cooking utensils are just too big. What you need is a basic assortment of small equipment. But there are so many sizes to choose from, it's sometimes confusing to know what to use. Here's a quick rundown on some common small-size equipment we used in testing the recipes in this book. To help stock your kitchen, choose at least one of each type.

Small saucepans: 1½-pint or 1-quart capacity.
Small skillets: 6 or 8 inches in diameter (also used for most crepes).
Small casseroles or baking dishes: 10-, 12-, or 14-ounce capacity.
Small bowls: 2- or 3-cup capacity.

Rye-Reuben Sizzler

293 Calories

1 slice rye bread
2 tablespoons reduced-calorie Thousand Island salad dressing

● Toast the slice of rye bread. Spread the toasted bread with the Thousand Island salad dressing.

Going on a picnic? Stick to your diet and bring along this sinless sandwich. Place the foil packet, bread side down, over medium-hot coals about 15 minutes or till the cheese melts and the sandwich is heated through.

½ of a 3-ounce package sliced corned beef
1 1-ounce slice mozzarella cheese
¼ cup sauerkraut, rinsed, drained, and snipped

● Place corned beef, mozzarella cheese, and sauerkraut atop the toasted bread slice. Place the sandwich, bread side down, on a piece of foil. Bring foil up and around sandwich to seal, as shown.

● Place the foil packet, bread side down, on a baking sheet or baking tray. Bake in a 375° oven or toaster oven about 15 minutes or till the cheese melts and the sandwich is heated through. Remove the sandwich from foil. Makes 1 serving.

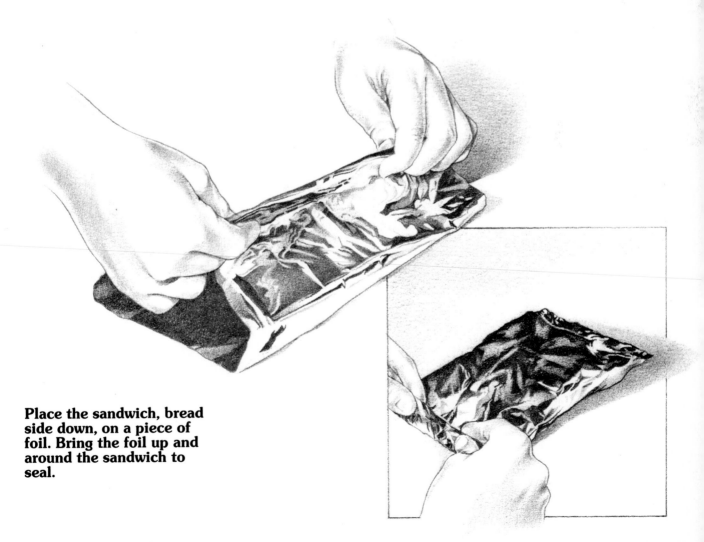

Place the sandwich, bread side down, on a piece of foil. Bring the foil up and around the sandwich to seal.

Potato-Vegetable Soup

270 Calories

1 medium potato, peeled
  and diced
⅓ cup water
2 tablespoons chopped
  onion
2 tablespoons sliced celery
¼ teaspoon instant chicken
  bouillon granules
⅛ teaspoon dried basil,
  crushed

● In a small saucepan combine the diced potato, water, chopped onion, sliced celery, chicken bouillon granules, and dried basil. Bring to boiling; reduce heat. Cover and simmer for 5 minutes.

Pack a small vacuum bottle full of this creamy blend of potato, ham, and vegetables for a hot and healthy lunch to go.

¼ cup frozen peas

● Add the peas to the potato mixture in the saucepan. Bring to boiling; reduce heat. Cover and simmer about 5 minutes more or till the vegetables are tender.

½ cup skim milk
1 teaspoon cornstarch
¼ cup diced fully cooked
  ham
  Dash pepper

● Stir together the skim milk and cornstarch; add to the potato mixture in the saucepan. Stir in the diced ham and pepper. Cook and stir till the mixture is thickened and bubbly. Cook and stir 2 minutes more. Transfer to a soup bowl. Makes 1 serving.

Chicken-Apple Soup

301 Calories

¾ cup apple cider *or* juice
1 teaspoon catsup
⅛ teaspoon salt
Pinch dried basil, crushed
Dash pepper

½ of a whole medium
chicken breast, skinned,
boned, and cubed
1 small carrot, thinly
bias sliced
¼ cup chopped celery
¼ cup chopped apple
2 tablespoons chopped
onion

● In a small saucepan combine apple cider or juice, catsup, salt, basil, and pepper. Bring to boiling.

● Add chicken, carrot, celery, apple, and onion to saucepan. Return to boiling; reduce heat. Cover and simmer for 15 to 20 minutes or till chicken and vegetables are tender. Transfer to a soup bowl. Makes 1 serving.

We've given an old favorite a fresh, new twist by adding apple orchard goodness.

Scandinavian Crisp Bread

130 Calories

¾ cup all-purpose flour
½ cup rye flour
1 tablespoon brown sugar
1 teaspoon caraway seed
½ teaspoon baking powder
Dash salt

● In a small mixing bowl stir together all-purpose flour, rye flour, brown sugar, caraway seed, baking powder, and salt.

2 tablespoons butter *or* margarine
¼ cup water

● Cut butter or margarine into the dry ingredients till the mixture resembles coarse crumbs. Add water all at once; stir till mixture can be gathered into a ball.

● Turn dough out onto a lightly floured surface. Knead gently for 8 to 10 strokes. Divide the dough into six equal portions; shape into balls. On a lightly floured surface roll each ball of dough into a 6-inch round. Prick the entire surface of the dough with a fork.

Nonstick vegetable spray coating

● Spray a baking sheet with nonstick vegetable spray coating. Transfer the rounds of dough to the baking sheet. Bake in a 325° oven about 15 minutes or till light brown. With a wide spatula, turn the bread rounds over and bake for 5 to 6 minutes more or till crisp. Remove from oven; cool on a wire rack. Makes 6 servings.

Serve these toasted rye-caraway crackers in place of bread for a new sandwich twist or as an accompaniment to a steaming bowl of soup. Tightly wrap and store them at room temperature and you can enjoy their crunch for at least 1 week.

Scandinavian Sprout Sandwich

292 Calories

2 tablespoons low-fat cottage cheese
1 tablespoon low-calorie creamy cucumber salad dressing

¼ cup shredded zucchini
2 tablespoons shredded cheddar cheese (½ ounce)
1 tablespoon sunflower nuts
1 round of Scandinavian Crisp Bread (see recipe, opposite)
¼ cup alfalfa sprouts

● In a small mixing bowl combine the cottage cheese and creamy cucumber salad dressing. Stir mixture with a fork till well combined.

● Add the shredded zucchini, cheddar cheese, and sunflower nuts to the cottage cheese mixture; mix well.
    Spread the cheese mixture atop Scandinavian Crisp Bread. Sprinkle with alfalfa sprouts. Makes 1 serving.

The Danish are well-noted for their fresh-tasting open-face sandwiches, and this slim combo is a good example.
    For a change of pace, vary the sandwich by choosing a salad dressing from pages 76-78. Or, try replacing the crisp bread with half of a pita bread round that has been split horizontally and toasted (see tip, page 35).

Sprout Gardening in a Jar

Many sprouts, like the alfalfa sprouts for the *Scandinavian Sprout Sandwich* above, can be grown at home. All you need is a 1-quart jar, cheesecloth, and seeds or dried beans. (Alfalfa seeds, mung beans, soybeans, lentils, and garbanzo beans work well.)

Wash and sort ¼ cup of seeds or beans, discarding any damaged ones. Soak them overnight in 1 cup of *water* (they may swell to twice their size). Drain and rinse. Place the soaked seeds or beans in the 1-quart jar. Cover the top of the jar with two layers of cheesecloth; fasten with a rubber band or string, as shown. Place the jar on its side so seeds or beans form a shallow layer. Store the jar in a warm, dark place (68° to 75° F). Rinse seeds or beans once daily in lukewarm water. Your sprouts should be ready to harvest in 3 to 5 days. Chill to store.

Once you've mastered the art of sprouting, don't limit sprouts just to sandwiches. You can sprinkle them over salads, soups, and vegetables, or put them in omelets, dips, and spreads.

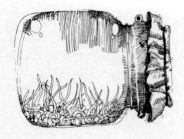

Spicy Beef Base

138 Calories per serving

½	**pound lean ground beef**
¼	**cup sliced green onion**

● In a small skillet cook ground beef and onion over medium heat till meat is brown and onion is tender; drain off fat.

¼	**teaspoon garlic salt**
¼	**teaspoon chili powder**

● Stir garlic salt and chili powder into the meat mixture in the skillet. Remove from heat; cool. Divide mixture into thirds. Spoon into three ½-cup freezer containers with tight-fitting lids. Seal, label, and freeze for up to 3 months. Makes enough for 3 (½-cup) servings.

This chili powder-seasoned meat base is the cornerstone for the *Tostada con Carne* as well as the *Burgundy Beef Soup* and *Parmesan-Beef Frittata* on pages 66-67.

To assemble the tostada, spoon the meat mixture evenly over the tortilla.

Then sprinkle the shredded lettuce over the meat mixture.

Tostada con Carne

275 Calories

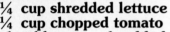

1 6-inch tortilla	● Place the tortilla on a baking sheet. Bake in a 350° oven about 10 minutes or till crisp.
1 serving (½ cup) Spicy Beef Base (see recipe at left) 1 tablespoon taco sauce 1 tablespoon water	● Meanwhile, in a small saucepan combine Spicy Beef Base, taco sauce, and water. Cover and cook over low heat till mixture is heated through, stirring occasionally.
¼ cup shredded lettuce ¼ cup chopped tomato 1 tablespoon shredded cheddar cheese	● Spoon meat mixture over crisped tortilla. Top with lettuce, tomato, and cheese, as shown. Makes 1 serving.

Use this recipe as a nifty way to make low-cal taco salad. Simply omit the tortilla, increase the shredded lettuce to ½ cup, and pile the meat mixture, tomatoes, and cheese on the lettuce. You'll have another great Mexican meal for only 216 calories.

Finally, top with the chopped tomato and shredded cheddar cheese.

Burgundy-Beef Soup

256 Calories

Pictured on page 5.

1 serving (½ cup) Spicy
   Beef Base (see recipe,
   page 64)
½ of an 8-ounce can (½ cup)
   tomato sauce
¼ cup shredded carrot

● In a small saucepan combine the frozen Spicy Beef Base, tomato sauce, and shredded carrot.

The beef base makes this soup easy and wine adds a touch of elegance. Top it off with a salad or sandwich, add a glass of skim milk, and you've got yourself a sensational lunch.

⅓ cup water
¼ cup dry red wine
1 tablespoon grated
   Parmesan cheese

● Add the water and dry red wine to the meat mixture in the saucepan. Bring to boiling; reduce the heat. Cover and simmer the mixture for 5 minutes, stirring occasionally. Transfer to a soup bowl; sprinkle with grated Parmesan cheese. Makes 1 serving.

No-Cal Thirst Quencher: Bottled Water

Bottled water is a smart choice for any thirsty dieter. Both domestic and imported bottled waters are quite different from the water that comes out of your kitchen tap.

Bottled water can be processed water, natural or spring water, mineral water, or sparkling water. Just as wine flavor depends upon the grape used, each type of bottled water gets its own distinctive flavor from the trace elements or minerals that are present in the water. You may want to experiment with types and brands of bottled water, since they do vary considerably.

You can find bottled water in liquor stores and on the soft drink shelves in most large supermarkets. To serve, pour bottled water over ice and add a twist of lime or a slice of lemon.

Parmesan-Beef Frittata

329 Calories

Nonstick vegetable spray coating 1 serving (½ cup) Spicy Beef Base (see recipe, page 64) 1 tablespoon chopped green pepper	● Spray a 6-inch skillet with nonstick vegetable spray coating. In the skillet combine frozen Spicy Beef Base and chopped green pepper. Cover and cook over medium-low heat for 5 to 10 minutes or till the meat mixture is thawed, stirring to break up the meat. Cook and stir till the meat mixture is heated through.	A frittata by any other name is really just an open-face omelet. This one's filled with spicy meat and sprinkled with Parmesan cheese. By omitting oil, using skim milk instead of whole milk, and going easy on the cheese, you shave off 200 calories.
2 eggs 2 tablespoons skim milk	● In a small mixing bowl beat the eggs and skim milk with a fork or rotary beater till well combined. Pour the egg mixture evenly over meat in the skillet.	
2 teaspoons grated Parmesan cheese	● Cook the egg and meat mixture over medium heat, lifting the edges of the mixture occasionally to allow the uncooked egg to flow underneath. Cook till the top is almost set and bottom is light brown. Remove the skillet from the heat; sprinkle with the grated Parmesan cheese. Makes 1 serving.	

Spinach-Parsley Pesto

37 Calories per serving

1 **cup lightly packed fresh spinach leaves**
1 **cup lightly packed parsley sprigs, stems removed**
1 **egg yolk**
1 **tablespoon olive oil** *or* **cooking oil**
1 **clove garlic, minced**
1 **teaspoon dried basil, crushed**

● In a blender container or food processor bowl combine the fresh spinach leaves, parsley sprigs, egg yolk, olive or cooking oil, garlic clove, and dried basil. Cover and blend till smooth. (If necessary, stop the blender or food processor and use a rubber spatula to scrape down the sides of the container.)

¼ **cup grated Parmesan cheese**

● Stir Parmesan cheese into the blended mixture. For short-term storage, transfer mixture to a covered container and refrigerate till needed. For long-term storage, divide mixture into one-tablespoon servings. Wrap each serving in clear plastic wrap. Place the wrapped packets in a moisture-vaporproof container or in a freezer bag. Seal, label, and freeze. Makes enough for 8 (one-tablespoon) servings.

Pesto is a popular Italian puree that is usually based on fresh herbs, olive oil, ground nuts, and cheese. By skipping the nuts, reducing the oil, and emphasizing the fresh ingredients, we've created a dieter's delight from this European specialty.

The natives of Genoa, Italy, who first invented pesto, insisted that for the best flavor, authentic pesto must be made by using a marble mortar and pestle (hence, the name pesto). But for speed and convenience, you can make this pesto successfully in either a blender or a food processor.

Pesto-Sauced Vegetables
(see recipe, page 71)

Pesto Pointers

Pesto is versatile enough to boost the flavor of dozens of foods. Start by tossing it with the traditional hot cooked pasta. Or, for a change of pace, try it with low-calorie spaghetti squash and chunks of chicken as we did in the Poultry Pesto Toss on page 71. And here's more: Add it to any of your favorite soups (see Quick Minestrone Pistou, page 70). Or, spoon it over a harvest of fresh steamed vegetables, either your choice of vegetable favorites or refer to our suggestions on page 71. We bet that once you've tried these ideas, you'll be ready to go it alone, inventing your own slim-and-savvy pesto combinations.

Quick Minestrone Pistou

227 Calories

1 7¾-ounce can semi-
   condensed vegetable
   soup
¾ cup water
1 tablespoon Spinach-
   Parsley Pesto (see
   recipe, page 68)
¼ cup uncooked
   fine noodles

● In a small saucepan combine vegetable soup, water, and Spinach-Parsley Pesto. Bring mixture to boiling; stir in fine noodles. Reduce heat; cover and simmer about 5 minutes or till noodles are tender. Transfer to a soup bowl. Makes 1 serving.

Presto! You can change ordinary minestrone soup into minestrone pistou simply by adding pesto to the soup for extra flavor.

Dining Out and Dieting

Do you feel as if your diet is in jeopardy when you eat out? Keep these tips in mind to help you keep the calories under control.
● Avoid fried foods and those served in rich sauces. Stick with salads, if you like, but beware of calorie-laden dressings. Sprinkle your tossed salads with lemon juice or vinegar, take along your own diet salad dressing, or order dressing on the side and control the amount used on your salad.
● Since serving sizes in restaurants are often very large, try ordering a hearty meat or seafood appetizer rather than a main dish. Then add a small salad to round out the meal.
● If you're ordering a cocktail, opt for no-calorie club soda, lower-calorie dry wine, or light beer. Learn to sip your drink slowly so you won't want a second.
● Order foods exactly as you want them—for instance, without sauces, salad dressings, or french fries.
● At buffet meals or cocktail parties, fill your plate with the lower-calorie items such as fresh fruits and vegetables. Take the smallest plate but avoid overfilling it. Eat slowly so you won't be tempted to make a second trip to the buffet line. Concentrate on socializing more than eating.

Pesto-Sauced Vegetables

Pictured on page 68.

73 Calories

4 carrots, cut into julienne strips	● In a small saucepan cook carrots in a small amount of boiling water about 10 minutes or till crisp-tender; drain.
1 tablespoon Spinach-Parsley Pesto (see recipe, page 68)	● Transfer the cooked carrots to a serving plate. Spoon Spinach-Parsley Pesto atop carrots; toss gently till well coated. Makes 1 serving.

Jazz up any of your favorite vegetables using *Spinach-Parsley Pesto.* You can choose carrots, as we did, or try ½ cup cooked broccoli, cauliflower, brussels sprouts, mushrooms, or a few new potatoes.

Poultry Pesto Toss

199 Calories

¼ of a small spaghetti squash	● Place squash in a medium saucepan; add water to cover. Bring water to boiling; reduce heat. Cover and simmer about 20 minutes or till squash is tender; drain. Using a fork, scrape the inside of the squash into spaghettilike strands, as shown. Set aside.
⅓ cup chopped cooked chicken 2 tablespoons Spinach-Parsley Pesto (see recipe, page 68) 1 tablespoon water	● In a small saucepan combine cooked chicken, Spinach-Parsley Pesto, and the 1 tablespoon water. Add spaghetti squash and heat through, tossing to coat. Makes 1 serving.

In Genoa, Italy, pesto is combined with fettuccine for a traditional dish called *trenette.* For a light main-dish spin-off of this, we've tossed the pesto with strands of cooked spaghetti squash and tender chunks of chicken.

When the spaghetti squash is tender, use a fork to scrape the inside of the squash into spaghettilike strands.

Versatile Oats 'n' Spice

35 Calories per serving

½ cup quick-cooking rolled
  oats
¼ cup toasted wheat germ
1 tablespoon brown sugar
½ teaspoon ground
  cinnamon
⅛ teaspoon ground cloves

● In a small mixing bowl combine rolled oats, toasted wheat germ, brown sugar, cinnamon, and cloves. Stir till well combined.

3 tablespoons orange juice
1 tablespoon cooking oil

● Stir together orange juice and cooking oil. Pour over oat mixture, tossing to coat. Spread the mixture in a shallow baking dish. Bake in a 350° oven for 25 to 30 minutes or till golden brown, stirring occasionally. Remove from oven; cool. Store in an airtight container with a tight-fitting lid. Makes about 12 (one-tablespoon) servings.

This healthy granolalike mixture is all that it's cracked up to be and more. Use it in the *Barley and Oats Breakfast* and *Granola-Berry Breakfast.* Or go a step further and sprinkle it over yogurt, on fruit salads, in soups, or atop desserts.

Barley and Oats Breakfast

268 Calories

¾ cup lightly salted water
2 tablespoons quick-
  cooking barley

● In a small saucepan heat water to boiling; stir in barley. Return to boiling; reduce heat. Cover and simmer about 15 minutes or till barley is tender, stirring occasionally.

¼ cup Versatile Oats 'n'
  Spice
1 tablespoon raisins
2 tablespoons skim milk

● Stir the Versatile Oats 'n' Spice and the raisins into the barley. Cook about 1 minute more or till the oats are tender. Remove from heat. Stir in the skim milk. Makes 1 serving.

Pacing is the secret to successful dieting. Be sure to eat three balanced and well-spaced meals a day—and that should include breakfast! Skipping one meal may do more harm than good and cause you to overeat at the next meal. A hot breakfast cereal like this one will keep you going strong till lunch.

Granola-Berry Breakfast

Pictured on page 4.

137 Calories

¼ **cup plain low-fat yogurt**
2 **teaspoons honey**
1 **teaspoon vanilla**

½ **cup fresh strawberries,**
 sliced
1 **tablespoon Versatile Oats**
 'n' Spice (see recipe,
 opposite)

● In a small mixing bowl stir together yogurt, honey, and vanilla.

● Place berries in a small serving bowl. Spoon yogurt mixture atop; sprinkle with Versatile Oats 'n' Spice. Makes 1 serving.

The crunchy oat mix combined with yogurt and strawberries—or any berries for that matter—makes getting up for breakfast well worthwhile.

Sprinkle *Versatile Oats 'n' Spice* atop the strawberries and yogurt mixture in the bowl.

Pick and Choose to Lose

Now's your chance to pick and choose the ingredients to build your very own low-calorie salad. On the opposite page are lists of possible salad ingredients and the calories for each specified measure. By using the lists as a guide, you can toss together your favorite salad and estimate calories at a glance. Or, pick up on the salad ideas that are shown and leave the calorie counting to us. Either way, you're sure to be a winner at losing. And don't forget our homemade low-calorie salad dressings—a great finishing touch for any salad.

Savory Tomato Dressing
(see recipe, page 77)

15 Calories

30 Calories

Creamy Italian Dressing
(see recipe, page 76)

55 Calories

Creamy Mustard Dressing
(see recipe, page 76)

145 Calories

40 Calories

5 Calories	10 Calories	15 Calories	Pile on Protein
½ cup torn greens	¼ cup cut green beans	1 small carrot	3 ounces cooked shrimp (100 Calories)
¼ cup shredded cabbage	¼ cup chopped green pepper	½ of a medium tomato	½ cup tuna, water pack (126 Calories)
¼ cup chopped celery	¼ cup sliced cauliflower flowerets	¼ cup broccoli flowerets	3 ounces fully cooked ham (159 Calories)
¼ cup sliced fresh mushrooms	¼ cup steamed asparagus spears	¼ cup steamed brussels sprouts	2 hard-cooked eggs (144 Calories)
2 tablespoons snipped parsley	¼ cup chopped kohlrabi	4 medium green olives	½ cup low-fat cottage cheese (102 Calories)
6 cucumber slices	¼ cup bean sprouts	3 small ripe olives	1 ounce cheddar or Swiss cheese (110 Calories)
5 radishes	¼ of a medium zucchini		

Creamy Italian Dressing

Pictured on page 74.

21 Calories per serving

¾ cup ricotta cheese (part skim milk)
½ cup skim milk
2 tablespoons lemon juice
1 0.6- *or* 0.7-ounce envelope Italian salad dressing mix

● In a blender container combine ricotta cheese, skim milk, lemon juice, and Italian salad dressing mix. Cover; blend till creamy. Transfer to a storage container; cover and chill. Makes 20 (one-tablespoon) servings.

Ricotta cheese gives this a pleasing richness—quite a treat for a diet dressing! Store the dressing, covered, in the refrigerator for up to 2 weeks. For longer storage, place dressing in a moisture-vaporproof container. Seal, label, and freeze.

Creamy Mustard Dressing

Pictured on page 75.

9 Calories per serving

½ cup plain low-fat yogurt
1 tablespoon snipped parsley
1 tablespoon skim milk
1 tablespoon Dijon-style mustard
½ teaspoon sugar
⅛ teaspoon ground cumin

● In a small mixing bowl stir together yogurt, parsley, milk, mustard, sugar, and cumin. Transfer to a storage container; cover and chill. Makes 8 (one-tablespoon) servings.

You'd never know cumin and parsley come from the same plant family by tasting them. Cumin has a hot, bitter, nutty flavor; parsley, a mild and fresh taste. Try them together in this yogurt-based dressing.

Honey-Ginger Vinaigrette

40 Calories per serving

½ cup tarragon vinegar *or* vinegar
¼ cup olive oil *or* salad oil
2 teaspoons honey
1 teaspoon grated gingerroot
½ teaspoon dried tarragon, crushed

● In a screw-top jar combine tarragon vinegar or vinegar, olive or salad oil, honey, grated gingerroot, and dried tarragon. Cover the jar tightly and shake well; chill in the refrigerator. Makes about 12 (one-tablespoon) servings.

You can purchase tarragon vinegar at specialty shops or the gourmet sections of some supermarkets. If you want to try your hand at making your own herb vinegar, see the tip box opposite.

Making Herb Vinegar

Herb vinegars can add fresh, low-calorie taste to foods. If you have access to fresh herbs, try making your own herb vinegar.

In a small saucepan heat 1 cup *white vinegar* till hot but not boiling. Place 2 tablespoons snipped *fresh herb,* such as *tarragon, basil, thyme, mint,* or *dill,* in a clean hot jar or bottle with a tight-fitting lid. (Be sure the lid is the original lid of a vinegar bottle or is made of glass or cork. The vinegar will erode any other type of lid.) Pour the hot vinegar over the fresh herbs in the jar or bottle. Seal tightly and let stand for two weeks to develop the flavors. Before using, strain the vinegar. Makes 1 cup.

Savory Tomato Dressing

Pictured on page 74.

5 Calories per serving

½ cup tomato sauce
1 tablespoon chopped
   chives *or* green onion
   tops
1 tablespoon water
¼ teaspoon finely shredded
   lemon peel
1 tablespoon lemon juice
½ teaspoon sugar
½ teaspoon Worcestershire
   sauce
¼ teaspoon prepared
   horseradish

● In a screw-top jar combine tomato sauce, chives or green onion tops, water, lemon peel, lemon juice, sugar, Worcestershire sauce, and horseradish. Cover the jar tightly and shake well; chill in the refrigerator. Makes 10 (one-tablespoon) servings.

"The flavors in this dressing remind me of a Bloody Mary cocktail," stated a Test Kitchen Home Economist. For a more fiery version of this spunky salad dressing, add a few dashes of bottled hot pepper sauce.

Poppy and Blue Cheese Dressing

21 Calories per serving

½ cup low-fat cottage cheese
2 tablespoons crumbled
   blue cheese (½ ounce)
1 tablespoon lemon juice

● In a blender container combine the cottage cheese, *half* of the crumbled blue cheese, and the lemon juice. Cover; blend till well combined.

2 tablespoons skim milk

● Add skim milk to the cheese mixture; cover and blend till smooth. Transfer the mixture to a small mixing bowl.

1 teaspoon poppy seeds

● Stir the poppy seeds and remaining blue cheese into the cheese mixture. Cover and chill. Makes 8 (one-tablespoon) servings.

A shepherd boy's cheese lunch lost in a cave started the blue-cheese-making industry, according to popular legend. When he finally found the cheese, it was streaked with mold but delicious. You'll get the same great flavor in this poppy-seed-studded salad dressing.

Zippy Thousand Island Dressing

19 Calories per serving

¼ cup plain low-fat yogurt
1 tablespoon finely chopped
   green pepper
1 tablespoon chopped
   pimiento
1 tablespoon mayonnaise *or*
   salad dressing
1 tablespoon catsup
   Few dashes bottled hot
   pepper sauce

● In a small mixing bowl combine the plain low-fat yogurt, chopped green pepper, chopped pimiento, mayonnaise or salad dressing, catsup, and hot pepper sauce. Stir till well combined. Cover and chill. Makes 8 (one-tablespoon) servings.

Spruce up a salad or sandwich with this dynamite dressing. Add as much "zip" as your palate can take by shaking in hot pepper sauce.

Breads for Spreads

Dress up any bread with these creamy low-calorie cheese spreads for breakfast on the run or a nutritious between-meal snack. To help keep the calories in line, use some lower calorie bread substitutes such as melba toast (1 slice, 15 calories), breadsticks (1 plain, 19 calories), or zwieback (1 piece, 30 calories).

Cheddar-Pimiento Spread
(see recipe, page 83)

Citrus-Mint Spread
(see recipe, page 83)

Savory Broccoli Spread
(see recipe, page 82)

**Confetti Cottage
Cheese Spread**
(see recipe, page 83)

Piquant Parsley Spread
(see recipe, page 82)

Piquant Parsley Spread

Pictured on page 81.

38 Calories per serving

1 tablespoon skim milk	● In a small mixing bowl combine skim milk and minced dried onion. Let the mixture stand a few minutes to soften the dried onion.
½ teaspoon minced dried onion	

½ of an 8-ounce package Neufchâtel cheese, softened	● Add the cheese, snipped parsley, and mustard to the milk mixture in the mixing bowl. Stir till well combined. Spread on desired bread or crackers. Or, serve with fresh vegetables. Cover and chill remaining spread to store. Makes 8 (one-tablespoon) servings.
2 tablespoons snipped parsley	
1 teaspoon Dijon-style mustard	
Desired bread, crackers, *or* fresh vegetables	

Turn this sassy speckled spread into a smooth vegetable dip by stirring in an additional tablespoon of skim milk.

Savory Broccoli Spread

Pictured on page 81.

12 Calories per serving

½ of a 10-ounce package frozen chopped broccoli	● In a small saucepan combine broccoli, water, green onion, tarragon, and salt. Bring to boiling; reduce heat. Cover and simmer for 3 to 4 minutes or till crisp-tender. Drain thoroughly.
¼ cup water	
1 tablespoon sliced green onion	
⅛ teaspoon dried tarragon, crushed	
Dash salt	

1 cup low-fat cottage cheese Skim milk (optional)	● Drain cottage cheese, reserving liquid. If necessary, add skim milk to the liquid to make 3 tablespoons total liquid. Set the drained cottage cheese aside. Place the broccoli mixture in a blender container with the liquid drained from the cottage cheese. Cover and blend till the mixture is smooth.

Few dashes bottled hot pepper sauce Desired bread, crackers, *or* fresh vegetables	● Transfer the blended mixture to a small mixing bowl; stir in hot pepper sauce and the reserved cottage cheese. Spread on desired bread or crackers, or serve with fresh vegetables. Cover and chill remaining spread to store. Makes 20 (one-tablespoon) servings.

The green onion, tarragon, and hot pepper sauce give this versatile spread its savory flavor. The Taste Panel especially liked the chunky texture from the cottage cheese, but if you prefer a smooth spread, mix all the ingredients together in your blender.

Cheddar-Pimiento Spread

40 Calories per serving

Pictured on page 80.

1 cup shredded cheddar cheese (4 ounces)
1 tablespoon low-calorie French salad dressing
1 tablespoon water
1 2-ounce jar diced pimiento, drained
Desired bread, crackers, *or* fresh vegetables

● Let the cheese come to room temperature. In a small mixer bowl combine cheese, salad dressing, and water. Beat with an electric mixer on medium speed till well combined. Stir in diced pimiento. Spread on desired bread or crackers. Or, serve with fresh vegetables. Cover and chill remaining spread to store. Makes 12 (one-tablespoon) servings.

Try this deliciously sharp spread on unsalted crackers, celery sticks, or zucchini slices.

Confetti Cottage Cheese Spread

15 Calories per serving

Pictured on page 81.

¾ cup low-fat cottage cheese
1 tablespoon lemon juice

● In a blender container combine the cottage cheese and lemon juice. Cover and blend till smooth.

2 tablespoons finely shredded carrot
2 tablespoons finely chopped green pepper
1 tablespoon chopped pimiento
¼ teaspoon dried dillweed
Desired bread, crackers, *or* fresh vegetables

● In a small mixing bowl combine shredded carrot, green pepper, pimiento, and dillweed. Stir in cottage cheese mixture till well combined. Spread on desired bread or crackers. Or, serve with fresh vegetables. Cover and chill remaining spread to store. Makes 12 (one-tablespoon) servings.

"It really looks like confetti!" exclaimed a Taste Panel member when this creamy tart spread was presented. It gets its good looks and great taste from green peppers, pimiento, shredded carrot, and dillweed.

Citrus Mint Spread

39 Calories per serving

Pictured on page 80.

½ of an 8-ounce package Neufchâtel cheese, softened
¼ teaspoon finely shredded orange peel
2 tablespoons orange juice
½ teaspoon dried mint, crushed
Desired bread, crackers, *or* fresh fruit

● In a small mixing bowl combine the cheese, orange peel, orange juice, and mint. With a small wire whisk or rotary beater beat cheese mixture till well combined. Spread the mixture on desired bread or crackers. Or, serve with fresh fruit. Cover and chill the remaining spread to store. Makes 8 (one-tablespoon) servings.

Use fresh mint for the dried form when fresh is in season. As a rule of thumb when substituting fresh herbs for dried herbs, use 3 teaspoons of fresh for every teaspoon of dried.

Dilly Deviled Egg

105 Calories

1 hard-cooked egg
2 teaspoons low-calorie creamy cucumber salad dressing
2 teaspoons low-fat cottage cheese
Pinch dried dillweed

● Halve the egg lengthwise; remove the yolk. Set the egg white halves aside.
In a small mixing bowl mash the egg yolk with a fork. Stir in the creamy cucumber salad dressing, cottage cheese, and dillweed; mix well.

Paprika

● Pile the egg yolk mixture into the egg white halves; sprinkle with paprika. Makes 1 serving.

If you're tired of snacking on carrot and celery sticks, try this "dill-icious" egg. It can double as a wholesome snack or as a sandwich or salad accompaniment. Plan ahead and hard-cook a few eggs at a time. Then you can keep them in the refrigerator for spur-of-the-moment fix-ups.

Vegetables in Blankets

101 Calories

½ cup water
4 3½x½-inch zucchini *or* carrot strips *or* 4 asparagus *or* broccoli spears

● In a small saucepan bring water to boiling. Add vegetables; reduce heat. Cover and simmer for 5 to 10 minutes or till vegetables are crisp-tender. Drain.

1 slice whole wheat bread
2 teaspoons grated Parmesan cheese
⅛ teaspoon dried oregano, crushed

● Roll out the bread to flatten. Lightly brush water over the surface of bread; sprinkle with the Parmesan cheese and oregano. Cut into four squares.

Nonstick vegetable spray coating

● Spray a small baking sheet with the vegetable spray coating. Place *1* vegetable strip or spear diagonally across *each* bread square; roll bread around vegetables as shown. Arrange bundles, seam side down, on baking sheet. Broil 3 inches from the heat for 1 to 2 minutes or till the bread is lightly toasted. Turn and broil 1½ minutes more. Makes 1 serving.

Wrap seasoned bread "blankets" around crisp-cooked veggies for an innovative snack idea that goes a step beyond raw vegetable munchies.

Place 1 vegetable strip or spear diagonally across 1 bread square; roll bread around the vegetable. Arrange bundles, seam side down, on the baking sheet.

Cornmeal Crunchies

90 Calories

¼ cup cold water
3 tablespoons cornmeal
¼ teaspoon onion salt
⅛ teaspoon chili powder

● In a small bowl combine the ¼ cup cold water, cornmeal, onion salt, and chili powder.

1 cup water

● In a small saucepan bring the 1 cup water to boiling; add cornmeal mixture. Cook and stir over low heat for 15 minutes. Remove from heat.

Nonstick vegetable spray coating

● Spray a baking sheet with nonstick vegetable spray coating. Use a wooden spoon or rubber scraper to spread the cornmeal mixture onto a baking sheet in a thin, even layer, as shown.
    Place waxed paper over mixture. Roll lightly with rolling pin to even out surface of cornmeal mixture, as shown. Remove waxed paper.

● Bake in a 325° oven for 35 minutes. Turn the cornmeal mixture over. Bake about 20 minutes more or till crisp. Break into large pieces. Makes 1 serving.

In the mood for something crunchy? Look no further! These paper-thin, no-fry snacks will remind you of corn chips. Since they lose some of their crispness when stored, go ahead and eat the whole batch—you can afford the calories.

Use a wooden spoon or rubber scraper to spread the cornmeal mixture onto a baking sheet in a thin, even layer.

Place a piece of waxed paper over the cornmeal mixture. Roll lightly with a rolling pin to even out the surface.

Popcorn Potpourri

The next time you get the between-meal munchies, fight back with one of these five popcorn treats. Just pop 1 tablespoon *popcorn* in a heavy skillet over medium-high heat using no oil. Be sure to cover the pan and shake constantly till all the corn is popped (makes 1¼ cups popped popcorn). Then simply toss the warm popcorn with one of these flavor variations, below and opposite.

Fiesta Buttered Popcorn (63 Calories)
Combine 1 teaspoon melted *butter or margarine*, ⅛ teaspoon *chili powder,* dash *garlic salt,* and dash *paprika.* Toss 1¼ cups warm *popped popcorn* (see tip box) with the melted butter mixture till coated. Makes 1 serving.

Lemon-Basil Buttered Popcorn (63 Calories)
Combine 1 teaspoon melted *butter or margarine;* ⅛ teaspoon dried *basil,* crushed; and a few drops of *lemon juice.* Toss 1¼ cups warm *popped popcorn* (see tip box) with the melted butter mixture till coated. Sprinkle lightly with *salt,* if desired. Makes 1 serving.

Parmesan Popcorn (73 Calories)
Combine 1½ teaspoons grated *Parmesan cheese* and 1 teaspoon melted *butter or margarine.* Toss 1¼ cups warm *popped popcorn* (see tip box) with the melted butter mixture till coated. Makes 1 serving.

Fiesta Buttered Popcorn

Curry-Coated Popcorn (63 Calories)

Combine 1 teaspoon melted *butter or margarine* and ⅛ teaspoon *curry powder*. Toss 1¼ cups warm *popped popcorn* (see tip box) with the melted butter mixture till coated. Makes 1 serving.

Green-and-Gold Buttered Popcorn (63 Calories)

Toss 1¼ cups warm *popped popcorn* (see tip box) with 1 teaspoon melted *butter or margarine* till coated. Sprinkle with 1 teaspoon snipped *parsley* and ½ teaspoon finely chopped *chives;* toss to mix. Sprinkle lightly with *salt,* if desired. Makes 1 serving.

Curry-Coated Popcorn

Green-and-Gold Buttered Popcorn

Mini-Cal Mocha Puff

Pictured on page 57.

188 Calories

½ teaspoon hot water
¼ teaspoon instant coffee crystals
1 teaspoon chocolate-flavored syrup

⅓ cup frozen whipped dessert topping, thawed
1 Cream Puff (see recipe, page 56)

● In a small bowl combine the hot water and instant coffee crystals; stir till the coffee crystals are dissolved. Stir in the chocolate-flavored syrup.

● Fold the whipped dessert topping into the coffee and chocolate mixture; cover and chill. Before serving, spoon the chilled mixture into the Cream Puff. Makes 1 serving.

We love mocha—the flavor of coffee combined with chocolate—and thought you might, too. So we made a rich-tasting low-calorie mocha filling and gave it a good home in our mini-cal cream puff.

Tropical Gingered Fruits

135 Calories

¼ teaspoon grated lime peel
1 tablespoon lime juice
2 teaspoons finely chopped candied ginger

¼ ripe papaya, peeled and sliced
1 kiwifruit, peeled and cut into wedges
Lime peel (optional)

● In a small mixing bowl combine the grated lime peel, lime juice, and finely chopped candied ginger.

● Place the papaya slices and kiwifruit in the mixing bowl with the lime mixture; toss gently to coat. Cover and chill the fruit mixture in the refrigerator for several hours. Before serving, sprinkle with thin strips of lime peel, if desired. Makes 1 serving.

Why not enjoy the leftover ¾ papaya for breakfast? Since papaya is low in calories (only 119 in one of average size), you can't go wrong. Just chill the ripe fruit, scoop out the seeds, and serve like cantaloupe. Garnish with a lemon or lime wedge to squeeze over the fruit for an 89-calorie breakfast treat.

Peachy-Orange Whip

125 Calories

1 large peach; 2 canned peach halves (juice pack), drained; *or* 1 cup frozen peach slices	● If using a fresh peach, cut in half and remove pit. Cut up peaches. Place the fresh or canned peach pieces, covered, in the freezer for 40 to 45 minutes or till the fruit is frozen.
½ cup orange juice 2 tablespoons nonfat dry milk powder 2 ice cubes	● Place the orange juice, nonfat dry milk powder, and frozen fruit in a blender container. Cover and blend till smooth. Add ice cubes; cover and blend till well combined. Pour into a glass. Makes 1 serving.

If you've ever slurped a creamy fast-food orange drink before, you'll swear this is its peachy homemade counterpart. Freeze the fruit before blending to make it extra frosty.

Plum Good Pudding

165 Calories

2 teaspoons cornstarch 1 teaspoon sugar ½ cup evaporated skimmed milk ½ teaspoon vanilla	● In a small saucepan combine cornstarch and sugar. Stir in evaporated skimmed milk. Cook and stir till the mixture is thickened and bubbly; cook and stir 1 minute more. Remove from heat. Stir in vanilla.
1 small plum, pitted and sliced	● Arrange fruit in a 10-ounce custard cup. Pour the hot mixture atop. Cover the surface with clear plastic wrap; chill. Makes 1 serving.

Maybe little Jack Horner, the nursery rhyme character, was on a diet when he put his thumb into a pie, pulled out a plum, and left the rest behind. He must have known that plums are low in calories and high in vitamins A and C.

If plums aren't available, try this smooth vanilla pudding over ½ *cup* fresh or frozen strawberries, raspberries, or blueberries.

Fresh Fruit Creamy

91 Calories (without fruit)

1 serving of desired fresh fruit (see list, opposite)

● If necessary, peel fruit. Slice or section fruit, if desired. Arrange fruit on a small plate or in a small dish.

2 tablespoons soft-style cream cheese
1 teaspoon orange juice *or* skim milk
½ teaspoon honey
Dash ground cinnamon *or* nutmeg (optional)

● In a small mixing bowl combine the cream cheese, orange juice or milk, and honey. Beat with a rotary beater till smooth. Spoon the mixture over fruit. Sprinkle with cinnamon or nutmeg, if desired. Makes 1 serving.

Pick a fruit, any fruit (as long as it's within your calorie limit), and top with this creamy cheese-and-honey dressing. Since the calorie count applies to the topping only, don't forget to add on calories for the fruit. Take a glance at the fruit listed on the opposite page for some fresh fruit ideas.

1 orange, sectioned
(64 Calories)
½ cup sliced strawberries
(28 Calories)
1 kiwifruit, peeled and sliced
(59 Calories)
1 small banana, sliced
(81 Calories)
1 small apple, sliced
(61 Calories)
½ cup seedless green grapes
(54 Calories)

Hot Blueberry Sundae

159 Calories

⅓ cup fresh *or* frozen
    blueberries
¼ teaspoon finely shredded
    orange peel
1 tablespoon orange juice
1½ teaspoons sugar

● In a small saucepan combine blueberries, orange peel, orange juice, and sugar. Cook and stir over medium heat till the mixture is bubbly. Coarsely crush blueberries.

½ cup vanilla ice milk

● Place ice milk in a sherbet dish. Spoon warm blueberry mixture over ice milk. Makes 1 serving.

This fresh-tasting hot dessert topping also can double as a chilled fruit spread on your morning muffin or bagel. And it's only a mere 29 calories per tablespoon!

Spicy Poached Pear

139 Calories

1 small pear

● Peel pear, if desired.

½ cup apple cider *or*
    juice
⅛ teaspoon ground
    cinnamon *or* nutmeg

● In a small saucepan combine apple cider or juice and cinnamon or nutmeg. Bring to boiling; reduce heat.

● Add the pear to the liquid in the saucepan, turning to coat with liquid. Cover and simmer for 10 to 15 minutes or till tender, turning the pear occasionally. Transfer pear and liquid to a small bowl. Cool; cover and chill till serving time. To serve, spoon the liquid over the fruit. Makes 1 serving.

Poaching is a good calorie-saving cooking method because the foods are simmered in liquids, rather than cooked in high-calorie oils or butter.

Apple-Raisin Cream Swirl

122 Calories

1 tablespoon raisins
⅓ cup unsweetened
  applesauce
¼ teaspoon ground
  cinnamon

● Set aside 3 or 4 raisins. Snip the remaining raisins. In a small mixing bowl stir together the applesauce and cinnamon; set aside.

3 tablespoons plain low-fat
  yogurt
3 tablespoons frozen
  whipped dessert
  topping, thawed
½ teaspoon vanilla

● In a small mixing bowl combine yogurt, whipped dessert topping, vanilla, and the snipped raisins. Spoon the yogurt mixture into a champagne glass or a sherbet dish. Spoon the applesauce mixture over yogurt mixture; swirl with a small metal spatula or a knife to marble, as shown. Sprinkle reserved whole raisins atop; chill. Makes 1 serving.

Just in case your willpower is weakening a bit, we've included this rich-tasting applesauce treat for a guilt-free dessert indulgence.

To assemble, spoon the yogurt mixture into a champagne glass or a sherbet dish. Then spoon the applesauce and cinnamon mixture atop.

Using a small metal spatula or knife, swirl the layers together.

Index

T-Z

Tips